EXPLORING THE SOUTHERN TRADITION

Exploring the Southern Tradition

20 ABBEVILLE INSTITUTE SCHOLARS

Abbeville Institute Press
McClellanville, South Carolina

EXPLORING THE SOUTHERN TRADITION

Abbeville Institute Press
Post Office Box 10
McClellanville, SC 29458

AbbevilleInstitute.org

Designed & produced by Shotwell Publishing, LLC

ISBN: 978-1-947660-22-9

10 9 8 7 6 5 4 3 2 1

CONTENTS

PREFACE

WHAT WE HAVE KNOWN as "the South" has been for four centuries a major part of the American identity. This is true whether measured by population, territory, history, or culture, high and folk. In 2002 a group of scholars led by Donald Livingston founded the Abbeville Institute to combat intellectually the ongoing campaign to eliminate the South from "America," a campaign now dominant in public discourse. Their intent was to defend, explore, and apply all that "is true and valuable in the Southern tradition," which they believe has a permanent and constructive role for the present and the future.

The Institute has grown to a fellowship of 170 scholars of philosophy, history, literature, political science, religion, music, and other disciplines, and of creative writers of fiction and poetry. They have been inspired by the Institute's mission and contribute freely their time and talents.

In pursuit of its mission The Institute has produced public programs across the land and has conducted 17 Summer Schools for college students, many of whom have gone on to higher degrees. The Institute also has a weekly podcast and an online library of about 1000 lectures and articles covering a vast variety of aspects of Southern history and culture.

This volume contains only a representative sample of subjects addressed by the Abbeville Institute and of the distinguished body of thinkers who have participated.

The Abbeville Institute logo shows the Palmetto tree, which made the fort on Sullivan's Island from which South Carolinians defeated a British invasion in June of 1776. The Palmetto's roots are exposed, symbolizing that we explore the historical and spiritual roots of our tradition and that our tradition is uprooted and needs fresh planting

— The Publisher

Symbols

THE WAR FOR SOUTHERN INDEPENDENCE: MY MYTH OR YOURS?

CLYDE WILSON

IN THE ANTEBELLUM ERA, Matthew Carey, Philadelphia publisher and journalist, was the most zealous and articulate advocate of a protective tariff to raise the price of imported goods so high that American manufacturers would be guaranteed a closed internal market that would provide them with growth and profits. He believed fervently that this was necessary to build a strong country. Being a refugee Irishman, he wanted the United States to have powerful industry supported by a powerful navy that could compete with the hated Great Britain for the world market in manufactured goods.

In 1834 Carey was an unhappy man. As a result of South Carolina's stand against the protective tariffs of 1828 and 1832, Congress had just passed a compromise measure that would lower the tariff by stages over the next ten years until it reached a revenue-only level. Carey penned an editorial warning the South that if it did not submit to future increases in the tariff, it would face the righteous fury of the North. He reminded Southerners that the North was superior in manpower and warships and that the long undefended Southern coastline could easily be invaded.

This is exactly what Lincoln's armies were to do less than three decades later. Note that Carey has nothing to say about slavery and that he aggressively wishes to punish the South simply because by defending its own interests it was thwarting his agenda. His son Henry carried on his mission. After the war of 1861-1865 Henry Carey was to blame the war on free trade. If there had been a consistently high tariff, he said, the South would either have been impoverished or else forced to become like the North and there would have been no war.

The great civil war was caused by free trade?

I get this from the brilliant dissertation of my student Scott Trask on the state rights, free trade, and Southern supporting men of Philadelphia, far more numerous, well-informed, and respectable than has been assumed. Throughout the period before, during, and after the war there was always a large part of the Northern population that agreed with the South on the issues. Far more numerous than "Unionists" were in the South and virtually lost to mainstream history. This is a vacuum in American history that this conference can begin to fill.

I thought about Matthew and Henry Carey a few years ago when 60-some historians in South Carolina presented a manifesto declaring that the Confederate flag atop the capitol building in Columbia should come down—because it represented slavery and nothing but slavery. And I thought about the remark of Charles Dickens, who had spent much time in the United States just a few years before the war: "The Northern onslaught on slavery was no more than a piece of specious humbug designed to conceal its desire for economic control of the Southern States."

Our 60-odd historians declared that they were not expressing an interpretation—they were stating an indisputable truth established by their expert knowledge. Let's leave aside the fact that most of those historians, if experts at all, were in fields remote from the period they were asserting knowledge of and had never read a primary document from the period. They had been told that the South Carolina ordinance of secession mentioned the defense of slavery, which was apparently all the evidence needed to conclude that the war was all about slavery and naught else. In fact, they were not making an historical judgment at all but merely asserting their membership in the exclusive club of true experts who possess so much more knowledge than the mere stupid and backward citizens of South Carolina.

Long ago and far away, in another age and another galaxy, it was thought that historians ought to immerse themselves in the primary sources of a period before making a judgment about large events, and even then that judgments should be cautiously put forward. And that genuine students of history should strive to be, as far as possible, independent jurors and not hanging judges. Be especially careful of moral judgments about the past, warned Sir Herbert Butterfield. Scripture tells us "Judge not, that ye be not judged." For historians, it is more important to understand than to judge, and we cannot understand all the circumstances that led to men's actions in other times. Too often, in calling something good or evil, we are really saying "I like this, and I don't like that."

I could spend all the rest of our time discussing how the historical profession reached its current condition, but that would take us too far afield into the minds of dead white European philosophers and revolutionaries, who created the mental universe in which so many American scholars work, whether they know it or not.. For a long time history was "philosophy teaching by example," that is, the account of men's actions as good or evil in relation to the health of their societies. In the new form of history, actions are not good or evil in themselves, but only to be praised or condemned to the degree they forward or retard progress as defined by ideology. One effect of this is that, like my 60-odd examples, historians do not care about the weight of evidence but only about cherry-picking facts to suit the predetermined theory. The duty of historians, they think, is to make a better world, not to tell the truth.

Good historians know that causation is a difficult concept and that the cause of any great event like the war of 1861-1865 is complex, multi-layered, and many-headed . Can one portion of one document like the South Carolina secession ordinance explain that millions of people engaged in an intense four-year conflict over an immense territory—by far the largest and bloodiest event ever to happen in American history and on this continent? The war began with the firing on Fort Sumter? But what caused that? And why was slavery at issue when it had been an accepted part of American life for two centuries? And what about the thirty years of conflict that preceded the firing on Sumter?

And so on backward in search of causes until we reach the great primary cause–Original Sin.

Let us grant that the secession of the lower South was related to a desire to defend slavery. It used to be customary to examine and evaluate both sides in a conflict. Our historians fail to notice that if slavery was a cause of secession that does not mean that it was a cause of war. Neither secession nor slavery in themselves necessarily called for Lincoln to raise the largest armies ever seen in this hemisphere and conduct a war of invasion and conquest against the Southern people. For that is precisely what the war was, an invasion and conquest of the South by the Northern party that had control of the federal machinery. This is a simple truth that seems to be totally absent from American consciousness. It never occurs to the historians or garden-variety American nationalists to even consider this. Their automatic and unrecognised assumption is that Southerners are bad people who naturally needed to be put down. If one looks at Lincoln's party in 1860-1861, even before the firing on Fort Sumter, one finds major spokesmen filling the air with calls for blockade, invasion, domination, the healthy purging of a little bloodletting, and the ruthless pursuit of Northern economic interests. That is the weight of the evidence, but what we always hear are a few insincere conciliatory words from Lincoln.

Forget the bosh about "restoring the Union." It had long been understood that the Union could not be restored by destroying legitimate governments in nearly half the States and subjecting their citizens to military control. The very attempt changed the Union into something else—something which might reasonably be described as imperial.

Historians have spilled oceans of ink to explain why the South was so peculiar—how it was so evil or perverted that it did not want to be governed by Yankees— who as all the world knows have only the noblest intentions, even when they are dropping bombs on you. I have long thought that what we really need to investigate was the North. It was the North that changed radically: the Founding Fathers, even Alexander Hamilton, could not have understood Matthew Carey or Abraham Lincoln The South expanded tremendously in territory but its basic social structure and beliefs remained the same. Some work has been done on the North in the era of conflict but a vast amount is still to be done. I recommend this wide open field of research to any young historian who wants to tell the truth and have his career blighted from the start.

Let's look at the Careys' assumptions about the Union. For them the national government was something to be controlled and its power used to carry out their agenda. The South was not made up of sister States and fellow citizens. Southerners were merely an obstacle who were blocking the agenda and should be pushed aside. The South was not entitled to its own life, its own interests and opinions, but was just raw material for the will of the North.

If I had to make one thing the cause of the war it would not be slavery. It would be this aggressive attitude on the part of the North. One Confederate wag observed that the war happened because Southerners were a contented people and Yankees were not. Southerners did not regard the Union as a weapon. They knew perfectly well that their fathers and grandfathers had created a confederation that was to be to the mutual benefit and protection of its members. They had agreed to no such an arrangement in which they would be merely instruments of others' purposes and have their society altered at others' will. When it was clear that the purpose of the Union was to be perpetually perverted, secession was a logical remedy. All this Southern statesman pointed out all along.

There is the famous exchange between Andrew Jackson and John C. Calhoun at the time of nullification. Jackson toasted the Union. Calhoun replied: "The Union, next to our liberty most dear." They almost never quote the rest of Calhoun's words: "May its benefits and its burdens always be equally distributed." Even advocates of the most extreme Southern position never suggested they had any wish or power to interfere with the North. They merely wished to be let alone. To this end, they showed for decades a willingness to compromise. Calhoun had readily agreed that the hated tariff should come down only gradually so that Northern interests would have time to adjust and not be too upset. And though he took a strong position on slavery in the territories, he always indicated his willingness to abide by the Missouri Compromise if the North would do so in good faith.

I suggest that the unexamined assumption that Southerners are simply evil people who don't count and who can be put down without need for much justification lies behind the discussion of the war to this day. In fact, having written a number of articles suggesting there might be something to be said on the Southern side, I am accustomed to email and mail messages charging me with treason and threatening me with the same deadly treatment that was administered to my ancestors. With such people, American nationalism starts to resemble fascism. The Confederacy is these days is routinely likened to Hitler's Germany. This is indeed a propaganda lie of the very worst sort. It was the North, after all, that gloried in conquest and superiority, created a police state still unmatched in U.S. history, invaded other people, and often treated them as subhuman.

Recently an historian, self-identified as a Christian and conservative, wrote in celebration of how the American people had always rallied in great crises—such as 9/11, Pearl Harbour, and Fort Sumter. Hold on a moment.

Pearl Harbour and 9/11 were sneak attacks by foreign enemies. The bombardment of Fort Sumter was preceded by a gentlemanly warning, there were no casualties, no civilians targeted, and the garrison were allowed to march out with honour and go home. Are Southerners not Americans? Are we just like Japanese and Arab terrorists, evil people to be overcome by real Americans?

Further, he is simply wrong about the response to Fort Sumter. There was an outpouring of public sentiment and some volunteering after that; but it has recently been shown that volunteering had as much to do with unemployment in the Northeast as with patriotism; after those first few months Lincoln always had trouble raising his armies. It could only be done by offering large bonuses and importing foreigners. Northerners numbering several hundreds of thousands bought substitutes, went to Canada or Europe, or otherwise avoided conscription. For many Northerners the war was simply a money-making proposition. This was affirmed by numerous outraged patriots and foreign visitors. The British journalist Frank Vitzelly reported from Washington: "The only persons who seemed to display any activity are the hordes of hungry contractors."

Here is another good subject that has not been touched as far as I know. Did the event at Fort Sumter justify an all-out invasion which immediately forced the choosing of sides by all who wanted peace and inaugurated a war of immense destruction? How about examining Lincoln's actions in the light of Christian just war theory, which would clearly show that the invasion of the South was unjust.

The fact is that a great many Americans believe enthusiastically a lot of things about the great war that are not true. This conference points to many subjects that challenge the predominant interpretation of the most important event in American history. I wish I had time to demonstrate how the theme of this conference could be vastly expanded. In everything I say I believe I am validated by the weight of evidence. In a subject as vast as the war of 1861-1865 you can find an example of anything you wish to find—the same is true of the institution of slavery and of Reconstruction. It is all too easy for a historian to cherry-pick evidence to support the established view. Of course, evidence does not necessarily lead to a change in beliefs that are based on powerful emotions and self-serving agendas. We can only hope that the cumulative weight of truth can make a slow inroad into false ideas. In fact, this is already happening to some small degree.

The North American War of 1861-1865 is still in many ways the central event of American history. It is unmatched in the scale of mobilisation, casualties, hostilities and material destruction on American soil, and revolutionary change in the American regime. The war, and especially Abraham Lincoln and emancipation, are perceived by many Americans and others around the world as the defining story of the United States, the essential myth that sustains the identity of Americans.

I am led to think about "myth" as a way of summing up historical experience by a fashionable notion bandied about in our day to interpret the losing side in the great war. This is what historians call "the Lost Cause Myth." In this interpretation myth is definitely meant pejoratively to designate something that is false and bad. The Lost Cause Myth claims to destroy the traditional idea, shared by many Northerners, including those who fought against them, that Confederates were brave, sincere, honorable, and heroic in their bid for independence and make a respectable part of the American heritage. This, they say these days, was all bosh made up after the war by Southerners to cover up their evil and failed actions. They were defenders of slavery and traitors and they lost. End of story.

Again, I wish I had time to describe the ridiculous falsehoods that are put forward to support such an interpretation of the Confederacy, which interpretation is discredited at every point by the weight of evidence. Perhaps next year's Abbeville Institute Scholars Conference could take up this theme. I don't think I have ever recommended to any group, even students, that they read my humble scribblings. However, I suggest you might join the Abbeville Institute and read some of the material in my archive that relates to what we are hearing these few days in Stone Mountain.

It is not unreasonable to use the concept of myth in the nonpejorative sense that myth is a story that is neither true nor false, but is an artistic way to sum up the meaning of great events of the past and the character of a people. A myth does not have to be precisely and pedantically accurate to be valid. However, I submit to you that there are grounds to argue that the American national myth is not true enough to qualify for myth in the nonpejorative sense. It is, in fact, a distorted and unhealthy legacy, an artificial concoction that lends itself to bad purposes. What these few days are about is to challenge and qualify this myth, and that is, alas, an uphill and thankless task.

I believe it can be shown that what Robert Penn Warren called the Northern Treasury of Virtue is full of wooden nickels and counterfeit coins. The American myth is demonstrated to near perfection in the 1940 film *Young Mr. Lincoln.* The handsome Henry Fonda, impersonating an imaginary humble and idealistic

Lincoln, is chosen by God and the voice of the people to meet the great crisis —to save the Union and free the slaves. This is ludicrously far from the actual moody corporation lawyer and relentlessly ambitious and crafty politician who had manipulated himself into a nomination. Not to mention that there might have been no crisis if he had not been elected and that 60 percent of the American people had voted against him, his party, his platform, and his potential to create conflict.

One of the historians who has been most zealous in putting forward the claim that everything positive that has been said about Southerners in their war of independence is a falsehood made up after the fact, does not understand why despite his wisdom and eloquence, people still continue to admire the Confederates. Why don't we see admiring books and movies about Grant? Why, people even write books about Lee's horse! One must feel sympathy for someone so impoverished in imagination and humane values that he can't understand why someone might prefer Lee to Grant.

I doubt if this will offer him much comfort, but I read that Spielberg is as we speak making a movie to be called "Abraham Lincoln, Vampire Hunter," to be released this summer.

The Forgotten History of the Confederate Flag

James Rutledge Roesch

THE CONFEDERATE BATTLE FLAG is, as John Coski of the Museum of the Confederacy titled his book on the subject, "America's most embattled emblem." Recent polls show that Americans are split down the middle on the flag: half view it as a symbol of heritage, half as a symbol of hatred (and an overwhelming majority are against tearing it down from public places). For all the outraged opinions, however, the true story of the Confederate flag - how it came to be and what it meant to those who made it and bore it - does not fit the narrative.

The first "Confederate" flags appeared in South Carolina in the months leading up to her secession convention. These early flags typically featured the Carolinian palmetto and crescent moon on blue or white fields. One such flag, which appeared in Columbia as the convention assembled, included an open Bible with the words,

> God is our refuge and strength, a very present help in time of trouble; therefore we will not fear; though the earth be removed, and though the mountains be carried into the sea. The Lord of Hosts is with us, the God of Jacob is our refuge.

When the convention relocated to Charleston, a banner featuring John C. Calhoun holding the broken tablets of "Truth, Justice, and the Constitution," with the caption, "Behold Its Fate," hung just down the street from the hall. Another Charleston banner depicted all the seals of the Southern States rising above a pile of the Northern States' seals, with the caption, "Built From The Ruins." When South Carolina declared her independence from the Union, a new flag for the newly sovereign commonwealth was needed. The *Charleston Mercury* described one of these sovereignty flags:

> The flag is a red field, expressive of defiance, traversed by the blue cross of Carolina, with the lone star at the intersection. The inner and upper quarter of the field bears the word "ready" surmounted by the palmetto.

The Charleston Daily Courier described another:

> When the first gun, "Old Secession," announced the secession of the State, they flung to the breeze the beautiful flag which now floats over their gymnasium. It is a red field, quartered with a blue cross on which is a lone star (others will be added as States come into the Southern Constellation). On the upper quarter is the Palmetto, on the lower a savage-looking tiger head.

The flag which South Carolina officially adopted, however, was a blue field with a white palmetto in the centre and a white crescent in the upper-left corner, just like South Carolina's flag to this day.

As more States seceded from the Union, sovereignty flags began cropping up everywhere. At the Alabama Secession Convention, the flag which hung in the hall featured lady liberty dressed in red holding a sword and shield with the caption, "Independent Now and Forever." Most States' sovereignty flags, however, were modeled after the U.S. flag, the "Stars and Stripes," as Southerners believed that they were the ones truly loyal to the foundational principles of American freedom. Indeed, just as the Montgomery Convention, where the seceded States met to unite in a new Southern Confederacy, adopted a Constitution which was modeled after the U.S. Constitution - though it more strictly limited the power of the central government - it also adopted a national flag which was similar to the Stars and Stripes, "the Stars and Bars." The

Stars and Bars was a flag of two red stripes, a centre white stripe, and a blue field with a circle of stars (one for each Confederate State). Letitia Tyler, the granddaughter of U.S. President John Tyler (now a Confederate Congressman) was given the honour of raising the flag for the first time. Harry Macarthy, the author of "The Bonnie Blue Flag," composed "The Origin of the Stars and Bars," a song which mourned the fall of the old Union and the Stars and Stripes while cheering the rise of a new Confederacy and the Stars and Bars. The idea of a "Southern Cross," however, stemming from South Carolina's early sovereignty flags, which were also considered in Montgomery, remained popular with the people.

William P. Miles, Confederate Congressman from South Carolina and Chairman of the House Military Committee, was the first to envision what would eventually become the Confederate Battle Flag. Miles regarded the Stars and Stripes as a symbol of "tyranny" and believed that the Confederacy should have a new flag. He designed a red flag with a blue "saltire," or "St. Andrew's Cross," lined with white stars. Red, white, and blue were "the true republican colors," explained Miles, respectively representing valour, purity, and truth. The saltire, according to Miles, was "significant of strength and progress." In fact, the saltire is the oldest symbol of sovereignty in Western Civilisation, first used by the Romans in Britain to mark the limits of their territory. Miles also found the Latin Cross of the sovereignty flags to be too "ecclesiastical," potentially offending Christians against religious imagery in war as well as alienating the Confederacy's sizable Jewish population; the saltire, by contrast, was "heraldic." The House Military Committee rejected Miles' Southern Cross as a Confederate battle flag, but at the Battle of First Manassas, it became clear that the Stars and Bars, when draped, was easily mistaken for the Stars and Stripes. This confusion led to some embarrassing incidents of friendly fire and nearly cost the

Confederates the victory. As a result, the military became aware of the need for a new battle flag.

General P.G.T. Beauregard liked Miles' idea of a Southern Cross for the Confederate battle flag, and convinced his superior, General Joseph E. Johnston, to avoid the bureaucracy of the War Department and create new battle flags themselves. Johnston ordered his chief quartermaster, Maj. William L. Cabell, to deliver 120 battle flags for each regiment. "My recollection is that it was an army affair," Johnston explained after the war, "and when questioned on the subject, I have always said so."

Cabell put his aide, Lt. Colin McRae Selph, an officer familiar with the environs of Northern Virginia, in charge of the new flags. After purchasing the red, white, and blue silk, Lt. Selph approached Mary Henry Lyon Jones, probably having made her acquaintance in one of Richmond's ladies' hospitals, established to tend to wounded Federals and Confederates. Mary sewed a prototype of the battle flag, which General Johnston promptly approved. Selph returned to Mary and requested her to rally all the ladies she knew to sew the needed 120 flags.

In addition to Mary, Lt. Selph also approached the Cary girls, who were all something of local celebrities. Constance Fairfax Cary had taken refuge in the Confederate camp after her ancestral estate was chopped down for firewood by the invading Federals. There, Constance met her cousins, Hetty and Jennie Cary, forced to flee from Baltimore when it fell under Federal control. Their cousin, Francis Key Howard, grandson of Francis Scott Key of "The Star-Spangled Banner" fame, was a Baltimore newspaper editor who was arrested for criticising Abraham Lincoln. In turn, Jennie set the words of "Maryland, My Maryland," the pro-Confederate ballad which is now the State anthem, to the tune of "O, Tannenbaum," and Jennie sang the song from her balcony in the presence of Federal troops. The Cary girls were daughters of the vaunted "First

Families of Virginia" - Constance descended from the ninth Lord Fairfax and Hetty and Jennie from the Jeffersons and the Randolphs. Hetty and Jennie were given the honour of drilling the troops and even formed "the Cary Invincibles," a group of the social elite in the Confederate army.

The ladies of Richmond, organised mainly by churches, set to work sewing immediately. Once the flags were complete, Lt. Selph took them to chemists and artists to have the stars painted. Selph's orders were to keep the project confidential, but as one lady remarked, "How could General Johnston expect four or five hundred female tongues to be silent on the subject?"

After a month of sewing, the ladies completed the battle flags. On 28 November 1861, the new flags were unveiled before the Confederate army. One by one, General Johnston and General Beauregard presented a battle flag to the colonel of each regiment, who in turn presented the flag to his color guard. Thomas Jordan, Adjutant General of the First Corps, made the following announcement:

> Soldiers: Your mothers, your wives, and your sisters have made it. Consecrated by their hands, it must lead you to substantial victory, and the complete triumph of our cause. It can never be surrendered, save to your unspeakable dishonour and with consequences fraught with immeasurable evil. Under its untarnished folds beat back the invader, and find nationality, everlasting immunity from an atrocious despotism, and honour and renown for yourselves - or death.

The Confederate soldiers loved the ceremony. "It was," recalled a South Carolinian, "the grandest time we have ever had." He remembered that "the noise the men made was deafening" and that "I felt at the time that I could whip a whole brigade of the enemy myself." A Virginian described the flag as "the prettiest one we have."

In addition to the mass-produced flags for the Confederate regiments, the Cary girls made special flags for their favorite commanders. Hetty chose General Johnston, Jennie chose General Beauregard, and Constance chose General Earl Van Dorn. Along with her flag to Beauregard, Jennie included an admiring note:

> I take the liberty of offering the accompanying banner to General Beauregard, soliciting for my handiwork the place of honour upon the battlefield near our renowned and gallant leader. I entrust to him with a fervent prayer that it may wave over victorious plains, and in full confidence that the brilliant success which has crowned his arms throughout our struggle for independence is earnest of future triumphs yet more glorious. In my own home - unhappy Baltimore - a people writhing 'neath oppression's heel await in agonised expectancy "the triumph-tread of the peerless Beauregard." Will he not, then, bear this banner onward and liberate them from a thralldom worse than death?

In his reply, General Beauregard expressed his gratitude and swore that Baltimore would be hers again:

> I accept with unfeigned pleasure the beautiful banner you have been kind enough to make for me, accompanied with the request that it should occupy near me the place of honour on the battlefield. It shall be borne by my personal escort; and protected by a just Providence, the sanctity of our cause, and the valour of our troops, it will lead us on from victory to victory until you shall have the proud

> satisfaction of waving it with your own fair hands as a signal of triumph, from the top of the Washington Monument in your own native city – Baltimore.

General Beauregard kept Jennie's flag for the rest of his life and had it draped over his coffin at his funeral.

Constance gave her flag to one of General Van Dorn's staff officers with a note of her own. "Will General Van Dorn honour me," Constance asked,

> by accepting a flag which I have taken great pleasure in making, and now send out with an earnest prayer that the work of my hand may hold its place near him as he goes out to a glorious struggle – and, God willing, may one day wave over the recaptured batteries of my home near the downtrodden Alexandria?

Van Dorn's reply brimmed with chivalry:

> The beautiful flag made by your hands and presented to me with the prayer that it should be borne by my side in the impending struggle for the existence of our country, is an appeal to me as a soldier as alluring as the promises of glory; but when you express the hope, in addition, that it may one day wave over the recaptured city of your nativity, your appeal becomes a supplication so beautiful and holy that I were craven-spirited indeed, not to respond to it with all the ability that God has given me. Be assured, dear young lady, that it shall wave over your home if Heaven smiles upon our cause, and I live, and that there shall be

> written upon it by the side of your name which it now bears, "Victory, Honour, and Independence."
>
> In the meantime, I shall hope that you may be as happy as you, who have the soul thus to cheer the soldier on to noble deeds and to victory - should be, and that the flowers want to blossom by your window, may bloom as sweetly for you next May, as they ever did, to welcome you home again.

According to Constance, General Van Dorn's staff officer told her that when he received her flag, he and his men all drew their swords and swore that they would honour her request, like knights of old.

The true meaning of the Confederate battle flag is not in the various ways which it has been abused over the years. Indeed, the Confederate flag is as innocent of its abuses as are other symbols which have been used for evil, including the U.S. flag, the Cross, and perhaps even the Crescent. The true meaning of the Confederate flag is in the women who made it and the men who bore it into battle. To them, the flag was not a symbol of racial hatred, but of independence and honour. To the descendants of those men and women, that is what it still means and will always mean.

Silent Sam and Me

Ben "Cooter" Jones

IN SEPTEMBER OF 1961, I left my job at a basket factory in Wilmington, North Carolina and hitch-hiked up to Chapel Hill to become a student there. I followed in the path of UNC's very first student, a boy named Hinton James, who had famously walked those roads up from Pender County back in 1789. As befits the first student at the first State University, he did not come by carriage.

My last ride was in the cab of a well-weathered farm truck. The grizzled driver wished me well and let me out in the middle of town. "You'll like it here," he told me with pride. "My little grandbaby went here and she became a schoolteacher!"

I was pointed the way to Battle Dormitory which faced Franklin Street, Chapel Hill's "main drag." My room, 8 Battle, looked out over McCorkle Place, the "upper quad" of the campus.

It was from there, over the next two years, that I watched the changing of the seasons on the campus grounds, the blazing autumn hardwoods and those seductive dogwood and magnolia spring-times, not to mention the passing coeds with their skirts, far too long in those days.

I was told that Thomas Wolfe, the author of *Look Homeward, Angel* had lived in that room, next to that same window back in 1916. I could not believe my good fortune in having landed in this "Southern Part of Heaven." Like Wolfe, I was overflowing with ideas and dreams and confusion. And like him I chased the elusive girls of the night and drank the last drop that was to be had.

The one constant outside that window, in every season, was the noble statue of "Silent Sam," the Confederate soldier who stood vigilant watch over the campus. "Sam" represented those young students who had left the campus when "the War" came, and who went off to do their duty. It was said that UNC gave more students to the Southern Cause than any other school. It is "likely" true.

Just a few weeks after my arrival, I joined thousands of other students as we tramped through the campus to Kenan Stadium, to listen to a speech by the nation's young President, John F. Kennedy, on the occasion of the University's Founders Day. Then in his first year in office, JFK was in full form, at his handsome, youthful and charismatic best.

And here is how he dealt with the South's past and the War Between the States. Here is what this liberal Democrat from Massachusetts said then of the Tar Heel State:

"There is, of course, no place in America where reason and firmness are more clearly pointed out than here in North Carolina. All Americans can profit from what happened in this State a century ago. It was this State, firmly fixed in the traditions of the South, which sought a way of reason in a troubled and dangerous world. Yet when the War came, North Carolina provided a fourth of all of the Confederate soldiers who made the supreme sacrifice in those years. And it won the right to the slogan, 'First at Bethel. Farthest to the front at Gettysburg and Chickamauga. Last at Appomattox'."

I was still a student at Chapel Hill when, a little over two years later, John F. Kennedy was assassinated in Dallas. It had a profound effect upon me. He had asked at Chapel Hill, echoing Goethe, "Are you going to be a hammer or an anvil?" Within days I was marching and demonstrating in the Civil Rights Movement. It was my way of dealing with his death.

The "Movement" was dangerous and heady. In the next few months, I was sucker punched, shot at, threatened often, and spent more than a few nights in jail during the sit-ins.

In the end, the Public Accommodations Act settled the issue, but those heady times were always a point of pain and pride when we all reminisced about the "the Sixties."

I had grown up in a railroad "section house" without electricity or indoor plumbing. The folks around us were in the same shape, except that they were all black. So I guess I felt I owed this to them, to those neighbors who got the short end of things.

That idealistic leap into political reality was the beginning of something else that was pushing to the front of my passions. During the summers of 1962 and 1963, I had a job on a work train clearing right-of-way along the railroads in the deep South. I loved it, every second of it. I began to realize that my Southerness was more than just a birthright. I came to believe that it was an honor bestowed upon me by my Maker. I still feel that way.

The period just after the Civil Rights Movement was critically important to the South. I remember how proud I was when a group of kids from Charlotte went up to Boston during that city's violent busing crisis to show the kids up there how to get along with one another. It seemed to me that left to ourselves, outside of any political climate, Southerners would get along as Southerners. For we had always shared a culture, that whole cultural menu of language and weather and food and music and work and laughter. We have far more in common than that which would separate us. That shared culture is being forgotten in these radical times.

Dr. Martin Luther King, Jr. never contemplated the destruction of historic monuments or the removal of historic symbols. His entire thrust, reiterated again and again, was for Southern white and blacks to "dine together at the table of brotherhood." He longed for the "integration" of our different "histories" as essential to our common future. A simple acceptance of the past is all that is necessary. With that comes forgiveness. It may not be easy, but it is necessary.

Fifty plus years ago I would look out at Silent Sam from my window in Battle Dorm and try to imagine what it must have been like to have gone off to war in those days. I thought of Sam as maybe a youth from somewhere like Tarboro or Clinton or Hickory. He was of good heart, I figured, maybe 18 or 19, a bit thin, a bit afraid. He was of that tough North Carolina stock, that "salt of the earth" fellow whose character is reflected in the State's motto: "*Esse Quam Videre*." To be rather than to seem.

He could have been my great great Uncle Gabriel Jacobs, who was killed at Frasier's Farm pursuing McClellan in his escape to the river. He was 21. He, in turn, was named for his great great great grandfather Gabriel Jacobs, a slave who was freed by his master John Custis in Northhampton County, Virginia in 1695.

Our South is a land of many secrets and many truths.

The radical trash who tore down Silent Sam and those academic idiots who enable them are not worthy to walk on the same ground as Gabriel Jacobs. Silent Sam will rise again, and we, not they, shall overcome.

Why Do They Hate the South and Its Symbols?

Paul Gottfried

THOSE SOUTHERN SECESSIONISTS whose national flag we are now celebrating have become identified not only with a lost cause but with a now publicly condemned one. Confederate flags have been removed from government and educational buildings throughout the South, while Confederate dignitaries whose names and statues once adorned monuments and boulevards are no longer deemed as fit for public mention.

The ostensible reason for this obliteration or dishonoring of Southern history, save for those civil rights victories that came in the second half of the twentieth century, has been the announced rejection of a racist society, a development we are persistently urged to welcome. During the past two generations or so, the South, we have been taught, was a viciously insensitive region, and the Southern cause in 1861 was nothing so much as the attempt to perpetuate the degradation of blacks through a system based on racial slavery. We are being told that we should therefore rejoice at the reconstructing of Southern society and culture in a way that excludes, and indeed extirpates from our minds, except as an incentive to further white atonement, the pre-civil rights past, also known as "the burden of Southern history." This last, frequently encountered phrase is from the title of a famous study of the South by C. Vann Woodward, who in his time was a liberal-minded Southern historian.

Arguments can be raised to refute or modify the received account of Southern history now taught in our public schools and spread by leftist and neoconservative journalists. One can point to the fact that a crushing federal tariff falling disproportionately on

Southern states contributed to the sectional hostilities that led to the Southern bid for independence. One can also bring up the willingness of Southern leaders to free blacks and even to put them in grey uniforms, as the price of the freedom that Southerners were seeking from Northern control. And even if one deplores slavery, this commendable attitude, which was also shared by some Confederate leaders, does not justify the federal invasion of the South, with all of its attendant killing and depredation. That invasion took place, moreover, in violation of a right to secede, with which several states, including Virginia, had entered the Union.

A comparison is drawn nowadays between two supposedly equivalent evils, the Old South and Nazi Germany. This comparison has entered the oratory of the NAACP and the Black Caucus; it has also appeared with increasing frequency in social histories that have come from the American historical profession since the Second World War. A bizarre variation on this comparison, and one frequently heard from the American political Left, is between the Holocaust and Southern slavery. First brought up by the historian Stanley Elkins (when I was still an undergraduate), this seemingly unstoppable obscenity is resurrected whenever black politicians demand reparations. Not surprisingly, those who claim that the Holocaust was unique, and that comparing it to any other mass murders, particularly those committed by the Communists, is an impermissible outrage, have never to my knowledge protested the likening of American slavery or segregation to the ghastliness of Auschwitz.

The benign acceptance of this comparison by would-be Holocaust-custodians has more to do with leftist political alliances than it does with any genuine reaction to Nazi atrocities. At the very least, reason would require us to acknowledge that Southern slave-owners were vitally concerned about preserving their human chattel, even if they sometimes failed to show them due Christian charity and concern. Unlike the Nazis, these slave-owners were not out to exterminate a race of people; nor did Southern theologians and political leaders deny the humanity of those who served them, a point that historians Eugene Genovese and Elizabeth Fox-Genovese have demonstrated at some length.

But all of this has been by way of introduction to the gist of my remarks. What interests me as a sympathetic outsider looking at your culturally rich region, goes back to an agonized utterance made by someone at the end of William Faulkner's magnificent literary achievement, *The Sound and the Fury*. The character, Quentin, who has journeyed from Mississippi to Cambridge, Massachusetts, to study at Harvard, and who will eventually take his life, tries to convince himself that "No, I don't hate the South." This question is no longer a source of tortured embarrassment, but part of a multicultural catechism that requires an immediate affirmative answer. That is to say, every sound-thinking (*bien-pensant*) respondent is supposed to hate the "real" South, as opposed to warm-weather resorts that cater to retirees and places commemorating Jimmy Carter and Martin Luther King. The South, as the location of the Lost Cause and of Confederate war monuments, is one that we are taught to put out of our minds. It is something that a sensitive society should endeavor to get beyond—and to suppress.

Looking at this anti-Southerness, in whose filter displaying a Confederate battle flag, particularly in the South, has been turned into a hate crime, one may wish to consider the oddness of such an attitude. Why should those associated with a defeated cause, and one whose combatants were long admired as heroic even by the victorious side, become moral pariahs for their descendants? Is there anything startlingly new about our knowledge of Southern history since the early 1950s, when my public school teachers in Connecticut spoke with respect about Robert E. Lee and Stonewall

Jackson, which would account for the present condemnation of the same figures? A few years ago, following my viewing of "Gods and Generals," a movie that deals with the personality and military career of Thomas "Stonewall" Jackson, I was struck by the widespread attacks on the movie director, Ron Maxwell. Apparently this celebrated director had failed to use his art to expose "Southern racism."

In fact there was nothing in the movie that suggests any sympathy for human bondage. In one memorable scene, for example, Jackson's black manservant raises a question in the presence of his master, about whether it is proper to hold a fellow-Christian as a slave. The devout Presbyterian Jackson, who ponders this question, has no answer for his manservant, with whom he has just been praying. How any of this constitutes a defense of slavery is for me incomprehensible, but it does confirm my impression that there is something peculiarly twisted about the current repugnance for the Old South- and indeed for any South except for the one reconstructed by federal bureaucrats in the last fifty years. On visits to Montgomery, Alabama, I have noticed two local histories, which, like straight lines, never intersect, but nonetheless confront each other on public plaques. One is associated with the birthplace of the Confederacy; and the other with the political activities of Martin Luther King and the distinctly leftist Southern Poverty Law Center. The headquarters of the SPLC, this watchdog of Political Correctness, stands obliquely down the street below the state capitol.

It may have been a pipe dream that the two historical narratives, divided by culture as well as race, could be either bridged or allowed to function simultaneously. What has happened is entirely different. One of the two competing narratives, the one about the South as a bigoted backwater until the triumph of revolutionary forces aided by the federal government changed it, has not only triumphed but has been used to drive out its rival narrative. It might have been a happier outcome if Southern whites and Southern blacks could have agreed on a single narrative that would not demean either race. The second best outcome would have been if both had retained their accounts of the Southern past, as separate non-intersecting ones that nonetheless remained equally appropriate for different groups. The worst outcome, however, is the one that we now have. It is one in which the descendants of the defeated are taught to vilify or treat dismissively their ancestors, so that they can demonstrate their broadmindedness and remorse about past racism. As a result of this inflicted attitude one is no longer allowed to speak about the South as an historical region without focusing on its real or alleged sins.

But this has not always been the official situation. Certainly this was not the case, even in the North, from the years after Reconstruction up until the second half of the twentieth century, when even veterans of the Union army praised their former foes. It was also not always the case even afterwards, as Shelby Foote's treatment of the losing side in his work on the Civil War, a classic that has gone through multiple printings, would indicate. The venting of hate and contempt on the South, as found in such predictably unfriendly authors as Eric Foner and James McPherson, is a relatively recent phenomenon. It underscores the fact that the Old South has been defeated twice—and the second time at the level of historical memory even more disastrously than in a shooting war that it lost in the 1860s.

The American white South has fallen victim to the "politics of guilt," a dreary subject, albeit one on which I have written widely. The Yankee victors of the 1860s, who overwhelmed the Southerners by virtue of their numbers and superior industrial power, did considerable wartime damage. They also subsequently occupied the land of those whom they had vanquished militarily, but then did something that was equally important. They went home, and permitted their devastated opponents to rebuild without an occupying army. What I mean to say is that the first occupation was morally and psychologically less destructive than the ever deepening humiliation that is going on now.

The first victors were mostly Yankee Protestants, who in some ways were similar to those they had invaded and occupied. Once the passions of fratricidal war had cooled, these Yankees were able to view their former enemies as kindred spirits. Although they were establishing a bourgeois commercial regime, one that differed from the prevalent Southern way of life, the winning side had also recruited farmers and those whose culture did not diverge significantly from that of those who had fought on the Southern side. In a certain sense Socrates' observation about Greeks once applied to Americans as well. While they could fight brutally with each other, they were still brothers, and so some form of "reconciliation" was eventually possible for the former enemies. And both North and South came up with a narrative about their past differences which bestowed honor to the heroes on both sides. This was possible with the Yankee Unionists, who wished to draw Southerners back into their community, even after a terrible war had been fought to keep the Southerners in a Union that they had tried to leave.

But the second civil war seeks the utter humiliation of those who are seen as opponents of a society that is still being imposed. The Southern traditionalists from this perspective are particularly obnoxious inasmuch as they are a full two-steps behind the project in question. Those who insist on these changes are no longer Victorian capitalists or Methodist and Congregationalist villagers from the North. They are post-bourgeois social engineers and despisers of Western civilization, a stage of development that these revolutionaries identify with discrimination and exclusion.

In Southern traditionalists they see those who are still celebrating a pre-bourgeois, agrarian, and communally structured world. That world appealed to hierarchy, place, and family, and its members displayed no special interest in reaching out to alien cultures. Such ideals and attitudes and the landed, manorial society out of which they came point back to a nineteenth-century conservative configuration. For our post-bourgeois leftist intelligentsia, this point of reference and model of behavior cannot be allowed to persist. It clashes with feminism and the current civil rights movement, and hinders the acceptance of a multicultural ambience.

The fact that people like yourselves are still around and still honoring the national flag of nineteenth-century landed warriors from the American South might have the effect, or so it is thought, of making others equally insensitive. Even worse, those who engage in these celebratory rites do not express the now fashionable "guilt" about members of their race and tribe. Those being remembered had owned slaves, and they would have denied women, whom in any case they treated as inherently different from men, equal access to jobs. Needless to say, non-Westerners are not required to dwell on similar improprieties among their ancestors or contemporaries, and so they may celebrate their collective pasts without disclaimers or reservations. The hair shirt to be worn only fits Western bodies, and in particular impenitent Southern ones.

It is against this background that one might try to understand the loathing that the political, journalistic, and educational establishment reserves for the unreconstructed white inhabitants of the South. You seem to bother that establishment to a degree that Louis Farrakhan and those unmistakable anti-white racists, who are often found in our elite universities, could never hope to equal. You exemplify what the late Sam Francis called the "chief victimizers" in our victimologically revamped society, an experimental society that fits well with our increasingly rootless country. But your enemies are also the enemies of historic Western civilization, or of the West that existed in centuries past. You may take pride in those whom you honor as your linear ancestors but equally in the anger of those who would begrudge you the right to honor them. What your critics find inexcusable is that you are celebrating your people's past, which was a profoundly conservative one based on family and community, and those who created and defended it. For your conspicuous indiscretions, I salute you; and I trust that generations to come will take note of your willingness to defy the spirit of what is both a cowardly and tyrannical age.

Confederaphobia: An American Epidemic

Paul C. Graham

Institutionalized Hate and Fear

A STUDENT AT FRAMINGHAM State University (FSU), located 20 miles outside of Boston, was "traumatized" when a Confederate flag sticker was seen on another student's laptop computer. This "bias incident" was quickly reported to FSU's "Bias Protocol and Response Team" (BP&RT) who quickly responded to the complaint. FSU's "chief diversity and inclusion officer," Sean Huddleston, responded with a mass email to the student population, explaining the details of the incident and strongly suggested that those impacted by the incident seek counselling. The BP&RT, said Huddleston, "will meet to determine any measures that may be needed to respond to this incident. Our primary goal continues to be to expeditiously address and resolve incidents that impede progress towards a welcoming and inclusive campus community." (Source: *Metro West Daily News*, Framingham, MA, 23 November 2015)

The irony of his position was apparently lost on Huddleston and other campus diversity enforcers. Some students, it is fair to say, are to be more welcomed than others.

The traumatization of the "offending" student resulting from this hysteria is unlikely to be addressed. Rather, we expect this individual to receive mandatory diversity and sensitivity training followed by a public apology and confession of his crimes before being expelled. Unwelcomed, unwanted, a persona non grata, this young student is but one causality of the hatred and intolerance characteristic of this disorder that is spreading at an alarming speed.

Cases like this are occurring all over the country - in schools, clubs, churches, cities, towns, states, and even at the federal level. A day does not go by without some new threat against persons, places, or things deemed "Confederate" or "Neo-Confederate."

WHAT IS CONFEDERAPHOBIA?

Confederaphobia is characterized by an irrational and pathological hatred and fear of all things Confederate - flags, monuments, graves, portraits, trinkets, stickers, etc. - *anything* that could be associated, even if tenuously, with the late Confederate States of America, including, in many cases, the region from which it sprang - the South, or Dixie - and those people and groups of people who are native or sympathetic to this region.

While Confederaphobia has long existed, it has been more or less manageable and - except in rare cases - did not openly target individuals and groups deemed undesirable or, ironically, in their language, "hateful," until the great Confederate Battle Flag purge that began in Columbia, South Carolina, this past summer. It has arisen from a small, rather localized hysteria to a national enormity.

WHAT CAUSES CONFEDERAPHOBIA?

In a society where Confederaphobia is considered normal and even virtuous, anti-Confederate attitudes flourish, thus creating a hostile and unwelcoming environment for native Southerners, especially if they refuse to renounce their Confederate heritage or abandon their outward Southern peculiarities - their accent and their manners, for example. Copperheads and right-thinking Yankees can also be affected. It is not necessary for one to actually tote a "rebel" flag or whistle "Dixie" for one to be bullied, ridiculed, or even targeted for violence - just the perception of Confederate tendencies is enough for becoming a target of Confederaphobes.

Sadly, this irrational fear is often caused by ignorance and/or arrogance, not pathology. Because this attitude is sanctioned by the educational establishment and reinforced in the mainstream media, many are convinced that they are sufficiently "educated" on matters related to the South and its history and, thus, are immune to the effect of any evidence or argument that runs counter to their ideological understanding of Dixie. Any evidence or argument is placed conveniently under the category of "Lost Cause Mythology" and "Neo-Confederate Revisionism." Once labelled thus by establishment "authorities," there is no need to consider the matter any further - no alternative interpretation is acceptable, no evidence that contradicts establishment dogma counts.

In this Confederaphobic society, countless Confederates and their descendants suffer in silence, as do Copperheads and right-thinking Yankees, neither of whom are immune from being bullied by Confederaphobes.

Most victims are afraid to admit to themselves - and to others - who they are and where they come from. They feel ashamed, guilty, and all alone.

VICTIM OF CONFEDERAPHOBIA?

If you are a victim of Confederaphobia, we can tell you with absolute certainty that you're not alone. According to some estimates, 80 to 100 million Americans are descended from Confederate soldiers. With the population of the US approaching 320 million, this would make 25%, or 1 in 4, genetically linked to the old Confederacy. Most people outside of the South are probably unaware of this "taint" and many inside the South know, but have been taught to suppress their *natural affections* and *normal* tendencies.

For most people it takes time to come to understand who you are and where you come from. It's okay to be confused, or to be uncertain about whether (or how) you should come out and live openly as a proud Southerner; to be who and what you are; to stand tall without apology or shame for your legitimate and praiseworthy history, heritage, and culture.

Education will be a vital part of your recovery as you move from victim to victor. There are many lies your teachers told you, many falsehoods that need to be addressed. As you become more versed in the true history of the South, your confidence will increase and your fear will decrease. There are many Southern-friendly resources and organisations out there that can help you along.

Remember

There is nothing wrong with you. What you are feeling is normal and natural.

STATESMEN

Calhoun's Meaning that Slavery is a Positive Good?

Donald Livingston

JOHN C. CALHOUN–valedictorian of his class at Yale, Vice President, Secretary of War, and Senator–was one of the greatest statesmen America has produced. Margaret Coit wrote a favorable biography of him in 1950 that won a Pulitzer Prize. In 1959, a Senate committee, headed by John Kennedy, ranked him among the five greatest senators in American history. Calhoun wrote one of the early works on the Constitution, and his *Disquisition on Government* was the first systematic political philosophy written by an American. It compares favorably with the classic modern political philosophies of Hobbes, Locke, Hume and Rousseau. Lord Acton (famous for "power corrupts and absolute power corrupts absolutely") placed the *Disquisition* in his list of the 100 best books ever written.

South Carolinians should be proud of this native son. Yet the politically correct in his own state seek to tear down the monument to him on Marion Square because he said in a Senate speech that slavery was "a positive good." Historians have distorted that comment to paint a picture of Calhoun as a dark, un-American character. And the distortion has created a fog that makes it difficult to understand what Calhoun meant. But if we pay attention to the historic context in which he spoke and to Calhoun's carefully guarded words, his understanding of slavery is in fact morally superior to Lincoln's.

The first thing to understand–which historians have long suppressed–is that slavery was a *national wrong* involving the

North as much as the South. New Englanders plied the nefarious slave trade for over 160 years. As of 1860, the wealth of America had come mainly from growing and shipping slave produced staples to Europe. The federal revenue was largely funded by this vast Southern export trade. As late as 1860, it was 75 percent of American exports. The North provided financing, shipping and insurance for the operation.

The greatest investment in America was in slaves. It stood at $3 billion in 1860. It is estimated that the North took 40 percent of every dollar the South made. Those profits were the seed money for the industrial revolution which would feed the industrial ruling class with a desire to remake the continent in its own image which it did by invading and conquering the South.

Since slavery was a national wrong, it demanded a *national* solution. The morally right thing would have been a nationally funded program to emancipate slaves, compensate slave holders, and integrate the freed Africans into American society. Yet throughout the antebellum period *no national political party* had proposed emancipation much less compensation and integration.

Integration was out of the question for Northerners. For instance, the constitution of Lincoln's Illinois forbade the entrance of any *free blacks*. Northern and Western states all had constitutional or legislative restrictions on free blacks entering. Companies were formed called "Ohio in Africa" and "Indiana in Africa" with the mission to ship several hundred free Africans a year out of those states until rid of the entire black population.

Lincoln won the presidency on the slogan "no slavery in the West." He explained to the voters that this would keep the region free from the "troublesome presence of *free Negroes."* (italics mine) When General Dix asked abolitionist governors of New England to receive 2,000 black refugees, displaced by Lincoln's invasion, they refused.

Upon first arriving in the Senate, Jefferson Davis was shocked to hear Northerners speak of the gradual extermination of blacks as a matter of course. They opposed slavery because, in providing cradle to grave welfare, it raised prices to unnatural levels. They argued that in a truly free market blacks would perish or immigrate to central America. This was a comforting thought to Ralph Waldo Emerson, abolitionist and one of the North's greatest writers: "The black man declines," he said, "It will happen by & by that the black man will only be destined for museums like the Dodo."

The *Republican* controlled House Committee on Emancipation Policy said in its 1862 report: "the highest interests of the white race, whether Anglo-Saxon, Celtic, or Scandinavian requires that the whole country should be held and occupied by these races alone." Historian George Fredrickson observed that Northern national identity "pointed ahead to the elimination of the Negro as an element in the population, through planned colonization, unplanned migration, or extermination from "natural processes." Recent studies show that Lincoln continued with plans to ship blacks out of the country a year *after* the Emancipation Proclamation and up to his assassination.

"Anti-slavery" agitation in the antebellum period, with rare exceptions, was motivated not by an intention to emancipate and improve the conditions of the African population but by a horror of living with blacks. Lincoln laid out the moral alternatives to his Northern voters. "What then? Free them all, and keep them among us as underlings? Is it quite certain that this betters their condition? ... What next? Free them, and make them politically and socially our equals? My own feelings will not admit of this; and if mine would, we well know that those of the great mass of white people will not.... We cannot then, make them equals."

So what was to be done about slavery? Lincoln could have done the morally right thing by explaining the need for a national program of emancipation, compensation, and integration. Instead he washed his hands of the problem. "If all earthly power were given to me, I should not know what to do, as to the existing institution."

Once the war started and got out of hand, Lincoln desperately proposed to the deaf ears of Congress a program of emancipation and modest compensation. But even then, he rejected *integration*, arguing that Northern states, like his own Illinois, should be able to prohibit the entrance of emancipated blacks.

As of 1860 the only group advocating emancipation were the abolitionists, a tiny fanatical group originating in New England in the 1830s. They demanded immediate and uncompensated emancipation backed by terrorist threats of the sort later carried out by John Brown. This was impractical *and* morally reprehensible because it failed to recognize the North's responsibility for the origin and continuation of slavery.

It was in this context of invincible Northern racism, inflammatory abolitionist agitation over slavery–but devoid of any morally responsible program to eliminate it–that Calhoun made his remark about slavery being a positive good. His purpose in saying this was to bring *moral clarity* to the issue. "Surely," he told Northerners, "if it [slavery as actually practiced] was an evil, moral, social, and political," as they said it was, then as "virtuous men," they were bound "bound to ... put it down." But this meant Northerners would have to shoulder their share of the financial and social costs of emancipation. And for Northerners that was out of the question.

This meant that whatever Northerners might *say*, they in fact saw slavery as a good, *given the alternatives*. Nor will it do to say Lincoln occupied the moral high ground because he thought of slavery as a "necessary evil" whereas Calhoun perversely described it as a positive good. The only thing that made slavery a "necessary evil" for Northerners was having to pay their share in eliminating it and having to live with free blacks. Neither of these objections to emancipation are morally commendable.

Lincoln and Northern "anti-slavery" critics are considered moral giants today because they voiced "opposition to slavery." But they were opposed to slavery only *ideologically*, as an abstract idea or principle, not as a *practice*–the latter they accepted. The strongest evidence that they accepted it is that they put forth no morally responsible national program to eliminate it.

Ideological agitation over slavery gives a feeling of pleasure that one is "standing for something." This feeling (which does not require doing anything) is confused with moral merit. But moral merit attaches only to what *you do* or seriously intend to do. To declare that slavery is wrong confers *intellectual merit* because you are saying what is *true*, but it confers no moral merit unless you do something to eliminate slavery. For the North that would entail a financial and social cost they were unwilling to pay.

The absurdity is that historians have treated Calhoun's remark about the goods achieved by the institution, which was intended as a criticism of ideology, as itself ideological: that is, that he thought of slavery as an *abstract principle* which gave some people at all times and places free reign to enslave other human beings.

Rather, Calhoun went out of his way to deny "having pronounced slavery in the abstract a good." And he gave an analogy to make his meaning clear: "Whenever civilization existed, death too was found and luxury; but did he hold that death and luxury were good in themselves." This qualification was given in vain to future historians.

Given these limitations, Calhoun argued that ideological agitation over slavery by abolitionists and their evangelical fellow travelers–which only distorted reality, created unrealizable expectations, unconditional resentment, and destruction–should cease and a fact-based study of slavery be undertaken.

Using social and economic statistics, he argued that slaves had arrived in a degraded condition, torn from their pagan tribal cultures into the most technologically advanced society in history. Gradually they had acquired the Christian religion and other practices of European civilization and were better cared for physically than Northern laborers who worked at near subsistence wages with no welfare benefits.

Historians today know that nearly half the children in New York City died before the age of five; whereas black child mortality in the South was about the same as for whites. Many had acquired valuable skills and some had nearly "kept pace with that of their owners ... in respect to civilization." He placed no limits on what virtues blacks could achieve, and urged that self-serving and destructive ideological posturing should stop and the Institution be nationally evaluated in another "ten years."

Calhoun thought it an achievement that slaves were gradually being integrated into Southern society through the plantation household; whereas Northerners perceived blacks as *aliens*, kept them out of their states and sharply segregated those within. Southerners for over two centuries had lived cheek by jowl with blacks and had developed reciprocal relations. Northern visitors often found this social intimacy offensive. It was, to be sure, a limited form of integration, but it was a morally substantial practice that in time could grow into something better.

Calhoun taught that liberty is a reward for virtue. From this it follows that as blacks achieved virtue, liberty should follow. Although gradual emancipation is implied in Calhoun's analysis of what he recognized as the *morally evolving* practice of slavery, he put forth no practical plan for emancipation. But neither did anyone else at the time, least of all Lincoln whose only practical solution was to keep blacks, slave or free, out of his state and the West.

Calhoun's wise counsel was rejected in favor of even more intense ideological posturing over slavery which made rational discourse impossible, tore the nation apart, led to a bloody invasion of the South, and an emancipation under the worst possible conditions for blacks and whites. An ideological style of thinking in the form of "political correctness" about moral and political matters–or rather, a failure to think–has captured American cultural and political elites with the result that rational political discourse has again become nearly impossible and the nation is once more being torn apart.

"THE UNSHAKEN ROCK:" THE JEFFERSONIAN TRADITION IN AMERICA

RYAN WALTERS

WHEN HISTORIANS DISCUSS reasons for Southern secession, as if the South needed to produce one, perhaps the most important, and sometimes neglected, motive was the protection of the Jeffersonian tradition, essentially the right to self-government. What was this Jeffersonian tradition or ideal? It is our lost political heritage of limited government and federalism, the political ideals that made up what might be called Jeffersonian conservatism. Those traditions came under attack in 1861 with the Lincolnian Revolution, which tried to kill it and has nearly succeeded.

The Jefferson tradition is a set of political principles, the true ideals of the revolution that Thomas Jefferson referred to as "the bright constellation" that guides our path. For Millard Fillmore, a one time Northern Whig, they represented a "beautiful fabric" and a "priceless inheritance." For Franklin Pierce, it was these ideals, embodied in the "unshaken rock" of the Constitution that could keep the nation from falling into faction and division, if they were adhered to.

That is not to say we have been free of political disputes, for they have always been with us and always will. With the ratification of the Constitution, America was very politically divided between two opposing factions, the struggle between the federalists, the "friends of the Constitution," and the anti-federalists, who opposed it. This battle spilled over into an ideological contest between two of President George Washington's Cabinet officers, which also pitted the two great regions against each other - Secretary of the Treasury Alexander Hamilton from New York and Secretary of State Thomas Jefferson from Virginia. This political fight began the two-party system and gave us our first two parties.

The Federalist Party, or Hamiltonians, believed in a strong central government, a national banking system, fiat currency, a national debt, protective tariffs and internal taxes, direct aid to corporations, loose construction of the Constitution, the suppression of civil liberties, and an internationalist foreign policy.

The Republican Party, or Jeffersonians (not to be confused with the modern-day Party of Lincoln), by contrast, believed in limited government, federalism, sound money, low taxes and tariffs, no national debt, government separation from banks, no subsidies for business, a strict construction of the Constitution, including the protection of civil liberties held by the people, and a non-interventionist foreign policy.

Simply put, the Hamiltonians believed in the merits of an energetic national government; Jeffersonians believed in de-centralization and trusted in the people to govern themselves.

During the Washington and Adams administrations, the first twelve years of the new arrangement, Hamilton set out to undo the limited government established by the Constitution, which he called "a frail and worthless fabric." As Hamilton once said to Washington, "we need a government of more energy" and that's what he sought to create by subverting the new Constitution.

Under Washington, Federalist arguments won out over Jeffersonian ones, at least on domestic policy. The government created a national bank (an early forerunner to the Federal Reserve), levied an array of internal taxes that included duties on land, alcohol, and even snuff, and began running up a national debt, which Hamilton believed would be a "national blessing." By contrast, the Jeffersonian Madison called a public debt a "public curse."

Now consider the great contrast here: Americans had only recently concluded a war of independence against Great Britain, with taxation being a major issue. As one historian has concluded, at the time the "revolution" broke out, American colonists faced a levy on tea that was so small that they would have to drink a gallon of tea a day in order to pay a dollar in taxes for the year.

And considering what Mather Byles had said of a possible break with Britain – "Which is better – to be ruled by one tyrant three thousand miles away or by three thousand tyrants one mile away?" – look at the situation Americans faced under the Federalists: In addition to state and local taxes, citizens now faced taxation from the federal government on several articles, which caused many to wonder just why they broke from Britain. This was especially true after the Whiskey Rebellion when the national government, under Hamilton's direction, used military force to collect these taxes. What had really changed? Some believed it was worse than it had been under the British. As Murray Rothbard has written, to the "average American, the federal government's assumption of the power to impose excise taxes did not look very different from the levies of the British crown."

By the time of the Adams administration, from 1797-1801, things had gotten even worse. In 1798, the government suppressed civil liberties with the Alien and Sedition Acts, a series of four new laws designed specifically to quash the followers of Jefferson. The crackdown on immigration was solely because most new immigrants from Europe were joining the Republicans, and many of the new laws contained sunset provisions that expired soon after the election of 1800. And the worst was the Sedition Act, passed just seven years after the ratification of the Bill of Rights, which punished political speech, so that the administration could, and did, punish Jeffersonian newspaper editors, including Benjamin Franklin Bache, grandson of one of America's most famous Founders.

This all proved too much for the American people. This was not the road they wanted to travel down. So in the election of 1800 Jefferson and his Republican Party won an overwhelming victory, taking the White House and sweeping both houses of Congress, a triumph Jefferson himself predicted, which stopped the big government offensive and killed the Federalist Party, for it never saw power again, ever. Jefferson called it the "Revolution of 1800," but one of ballots, not bullets.

As the new President, Jefferson immediately instituted what he termed in his first inaugural address as "a wise and frugal Government, which shall restrain men from injuring one another, shall leave them otherwise free to regulate their own pursuits of industry and improvement, and shall not take from the mouth of labor the bread it has earned." "This," he said, "is the sum of good government." He then laid out what he considered the "essential principles of our Government":

> Equal and exact justice to all men, of whatever state or persuasion, religious or political; peace, commerce, and honest friendship with all nations, entangling alliances with none; the support of the State governments in all their rights, as the most competent administrations for our domestic concerns and the surest bulwarks against anti-republican tendencies; the preservation of the General Government in its whole constitutional vigor, as the sheet anchor of our peace at home and safety abroad; a jealous care of the right of election by the people — a mild and safe corrective of abuses which are lopped by the sword of revolution

> where peaceable remedies are unprovided; absolute acquiescence in the decisions of the majority, the vital principle of republics, from which is no appeal but to force, the vital principle and immediate parent of despotism; a well-disciplined militia, our best reliance in peace and for the first moments of war till regulars may relieve them; the supremacy of the civil over the military authority; economy in the public expense, that labor may be lightly burthened; the honest payment of our debts and sacred preservation of the public faith; encouragement of agriculture, and of commerce as its handmaid; the diffusion of information and arraignment of all abuses at the bar of the public reason; freedom of religion; freedom of the press, and freedom of person under the protection of the habeas corpus, and trial by juries impartially selected.

Jefferson concluded with these words:

> These principles form the bright constellation which has gone before us and guided our steps through an age of revolution and reformation. The wisdom of our sages and blood of our heroes have been devoted to their attainment. They should be the creed of our political faith, the text of civic instruction, the touchstone by which to try the services of those we trust; and should we wander from them in moments of error or of alarm, let us hasten to retrace our steps and to regain the road which alone leads to peace, liberty, and safety.

As President, Jefferson put all those principles into practice. He cut spending, eliminated all internal taxes, repealed the Alien and Sedition Acts, and pardoned all those prosecuted under it, including the return of fine money out of the treasury. By the time he left the presidency in 1809, all of Hamilton's taxes had been abolished, to prevent what he called "the bottomless abyss of public money." The federal budget under the Federalists amounted to some $5 million per year. President Jefferson cut this by more than half, to $2.4 million. The national debt was reduced from $80 million to $57 million. In addition, the treasury accumulated a surplus of $14 million.

But he also did something else to totally change the nature of the government - changing its appearance.

In Jefferson's opinion the office of President had already taken on the style of a monarch, which is what Hamilton desired, so he ended practices that remotely resembled a king, such as the practice of publicly delivering the annual message to Congress.

His predecessors had certainly played the part. Washington dressed gracefully for his ceremony and arrived in a fancy carriage pulled by a team of six white horses. His entourage included marching bands and formations of soldiers. Adams arrived at his ceremony in 1797 in a more modest but elegant carriage with two horses. He wore a grey broadcloth suit, but topped it off with an elegant sword. His hair was also well powdered in the finest aristocratic tradition. Adams loved the trappings of high office and had even wanted to give the President an elegant title befitting that of a king - "His Highness the President of the United States and Defender of the Rights of the Same."

By contrast, Jefferson wore a simple suit, no powdered wig, and with shoes that laced rather than with a buckle, which he felt was too aristocratic. He walked to the Capitol for his inauguration rather than in a horse-drawn carriage. Residing in the mansion, he opened the door himself when someone knocked, even in his night attire, and removed the large rectangular dining table in favor of a circular one so that everyone present would be considered equal.

He also served his guests personally, rather than have a servant do it. These changes may seem trivial and inconsequential but it ushered in an era of republican simplicity for the country and fit perfectly with the Jeffersonian ideal.

Over the next sixty years, with only a few exceptions, the nation was governed by these Jeffersonian principles, operating eventually in what would become the modern Democratic Party. Though it took some time, the Jeffersonians eventually repealed Hamilton's entire program, including the ultimate destruction of the Bank of the United States and the elimination of the national debt under Andrew Jackson. Jeffersonian America was the freest and most prosperous place on Earth. There were no federal taxes on the people, no regulations, no federal police force, and no standing army. Americans had soundly rejected the centralizing ideas of Hamilton and the Federalists, and determined that Jefferson carried the sacred fire of liberty, the true ideals of the revolution.

Although Jeffersonian ideals governed the country for those sixty years, it's easy for us to sometimes refer to them as "Southern conservatism" or a "Southern philosophy," for Southerners largely crafted them and upheld them. But we must not forget that these were actually American ideals, American principles, and American policies because most Americans believed in them. And even though it was the South that early on dominated national affairs, electing a majority of Presidents, House Speakers, and other national leaders, and, by 1860, dominated the Supreme Court, there were many in the North that held strongly to Jeffersonian ideals, including many Presidents and other leaders. The only real nationalist President during the Jeffersonian years was John Quincy Adams of Massachusetts, whose very election was the result of corruption and who only served one term. Even many Northerners rejected Adams and nationalism.

As Eugene Genovese has written, "The state-rights interpretation of the Constitution has always had numerous supporters in the North. Southerners never ceased to remind their Yankee tormentors that not only state rights but secessionist doctrine had played well in New England well before the Hartford Convention. If anything, regional particularism and state rights doctrine were stronger in the North than in the South until after the War of 1812."

Despite Jeffersonian dominance, the great political divide in the country remained. Some portray the rift as a Jeffersonian vs. Hamiltonian contest, but since Lincoln brought Hamilton's vision to fruition, and as Don Livingston has so masterfully pointed out, the two competing visions for the nation are, in actuality, Jeffersonian America vs. Lincolnian America.

These vast differences were reflected in their political philosophies - the way they believed the country should be governed as well as the foundation upon which it rested. Jeffersonians believed in a decentralized state, a Union, or compact among the states, where sovereignty rested with the people of the states, and it was those sovereign states that came together to create the Constitution, delegating certain enumerated powers to a new federal government, while retaining all other powers for themselves and always with the understanding that those delegated powers could be recalled at any time.

These ideas are what most Americans, not just Southerners, understood as absolute political truth. William Rawle, a very prominent attorney from Philadelphia, wrote a book called *A View of the Constitution* in 1825, a textbook used most notably at West Point. He remarked that the "Union is an association of the people of republics; its preservation is calculated to depend on the preservation of those republics." Referring to the Union as a "compact," he writes, "The secession of a state from the Union depends on the will of the people of such state." In other words, it's not the will of the national government or the will of all the American people.

Lincolnians - people like Lincoln, Daniel Webster, Joseph Story - believed in the concept of a perpetual National Union, whereby the whole of the American people, who they believed created and empowered the Constitution, were deemed sovereign and the states were nothing more than provinces to be dominated and controlled by a central authority, a view that did not really exist until the 1830s. As Kenneth Stampp has written, the Jeffersonian idea of "state sovereignty and a constitutional right of secession flourished for forty years before a comparable case for a perpetual union had been devised."

And it was the system of state sovereignty, supported by nullification and secession, that could preserve and peaceably keep the Union together. John C. Calhoun contended "that the great conservative principle of our system is in the people of the States, as parties to the Constitutional compact." Senator Willie P. Mangum of North Carolina, an Anti-Jackson candidate for President in 1836, agreed with Calhoun, writing in 1834 to a friend and fellow Southerner that the "principles that you and I hold to be the only conservative principles of our Federative system, so far from having taken root in the North & the East, are scarcely comprehended by the most intelligent of the National republicans," which, as you know, were the forerunners to the Whigs and the ideological heirs of Hamilton. "The basis of all party organization in the North & East is naked interest," he continued. "Principles are silly things as contradistinguished from pecuniary interest." New England has a principle, he said, "that we abhor, & believe to be destructive ultimately of our system, in case it shall prevail."

And that abhorrent principle was centralization, or nationalism. This push toward the creation of a centralized state began with the increase of the New England Yankee, as a distinct group of people in both numbers and influence. Yankees were the polar opposite of Jeffersonians.

The Northern intellectual, Orestes Brownson, understood the mindset of the New England Yankee:

> The New Englander has excellent points, but is restless in body and mind, always scheming, always in motion, never satisfied with what he has, and always seeking to make all the world like himself, or as uneasy as himself. He is smart, seldom great; educated, but seldom learned; active in mind, but rarely a profound thinker; religious, but thoroughly materialistic: his worship is rendered in a temple founded on Mammon, and he expects to be carried to heaven in a softly-cushioned railway car, with his sins carefully checked and deposited in the baggage crate with his other luggage to be duly delivered when he has reached his destination. He is philanthropic, but makes his philanthropy his excuse for meddling with everybody's business as if it were his own, and under pretense of promoting religion and morality, he wars against every generous and natural instinct, and aggravates the very evils he seeks to cure.

This perfectly describes the Hamiltonian, and later Lincolnian, mindset. This is especially true of the abolitionists, who sought, through their magnanimity, to reach down into Southern states, immediately abolish slavery, upset the entirety of Southern society, without so much as a ripple of disruption to the North. And it was not because they cared about enslaved blacks in the South. As Salmon P. Chase said in 1859, "I do not wish to have the slave emancipated because I love him, but because I hate his master."

That should tell you a lot. It was about destroying the Jeffersonian South.

Jeffersonians as a whole, and Southerners in particular, never sought to do this to the North, unlike Northern conspiracy theories of the day. As Calhoun once asked, "When did the South ever lay her hand upon the North?"

By the 1850s and 1860s, this view was becoming widespread and the differences between the two pervasive philosophies more apparent. As Professor Clyde Wilson has written, in a fabulous book entitled *The Yankee Problem: An American Dilemma*, the

> North had been Yankeeized, for the most part quietly, by control of churches, schools, and other cultural institutions, and by whipping up a frenzy of paranoia about the alleged plot of the South to spread slavery to the North, which was as imaginary as Jefferson's guillotine.

This idea that the South sought to push slavery into the North is the main conspiracy theory they used to frighten people, which was exactly the theme of Lincoln's famous 1858 "House Divided" speech. As James Henley Thornwell of South Carolina wrote in 1859, "There is at work in this land a Yankee spirit and an American spirit." And that Yankee spirit, decidedly un-American, was working against the Jeffersonian ideal.

Jefferson, as politically astute as he was, saw these differences very early and wrote about them more than six decades before secession, during the darkest days of the Adams administration, to which he served as Vice President. To his friend John Taylor of Caroline, Jefferson wrote, in his famous "reign of witches" letter in 1798, the year of the Alien and Sedition Acts, that the young country was "completely under that saddle of Massachusetts and Connecticut," he said, who "ride us very hard, cruelly insulting our feelings, as well as exhausting our strength and substance." New

Englanders, he wrote in agreement with what Brownson would write 66 years later, displayed a great "perversity of character," which was a main reason for the "natural division of our parties."

And by the 1850s the meddling of the New England Yankee was creeping in and there are many examples of this but consider one bill passed in 1854 during the presidency of a great Jeffersonian, Franklin Pierce. Most people have heard of this story, a proposal to provide help for the mentally insane, and Pierce's reaction to it, but it was far from that simple. The law, passed by Congress and sent to the President, went much farther in how that help was allocated.

First, the bill would grant 10 million acres of land to the states; the federal government then set the per-acre price for the sale of the land, a dollar per acre, and if that price was not met, the land went back under federal control; the expenses for the care and management of the land was to be paid by the states; the proceeds for the sale and use of the land then had to be invested in "safe stocks," which could never be sold, and the interest gained from those stocks would be used to treat the mentally insane.

Pierce, a Northerner, objected to every aspect of the bill:

> It can not be questioned that if Congress has power to make provision for the indigent insane without the limits of this District it has the same power to provide for the indigent who are not insane, and thus to transfer to the Federal Government the charge of all the poor in all the States," he wrote in his veto message. "I readily and, I trust, feelingly acknowledge the duty incumbent on us all as men and citizens, and as among the highest and holiest of our duties, to provide for those who, in the mysterious order of Providence, are subject to want and to disease of body or mind; but I can not find any authority in the Constitution for making the

> Federal Government the great almoner of public charity throughout the United States. To do so would, in my judgment, be contrary to the letter and spirit of the Constitution and subversive of the whole theory upon which the Union of these States is founded. ... With this aim and to this end the fathers of the Republic framed the Constitution, in and by which the independent and sovereign States united themselves for certain specified objects and purposes, and for those only, leaving all [other] powers ... with the States.

Yet Pierce is today derided as one of America's worst Presidents.

This growing philosophical divide eventually came to a head with the emergence of a purely sectional party, the new Republican Party, conceived in 1854 after passage of the Kansas-Nebraska Act. The party grew rapidly by coalescing many different elements into it: old Northern Whigs, various abolitionist parties, and anti-Nebraska Democrats. The South certainly saw the dangers apparent with the Republicans but some Northerners did as well.

"If this sectional party succeeds," wrote Millard Fillmore to James Buchanan in 1856, "it leads inevitably to the destruction of this beautiful fabric reared by our forefathers, cemented by their blood, and bequeathed to us, a priceless inheritance." During his presidency, also derided by historians, Franklin Pierce realized what Fillmore did about the new party and the divisions it would cause. "The storm of frenzy and faction must inevitably dash itself in vain against the unshaken rock of the Constitution," he said. In other words, if we stick to our ideals, embodied in the Constitution, we will survive the political storms that lay ahead.

But that was the problem - Would the Republicans follow the Constitution? Many Northern Yankees had already demonstrated a propensity toward lawlessness and interpreting the Constitution any way they chose, reserving the right to violate it for the noblest of reasons, an attitude described by Brownson.

The new Republican Party nominated a presidential candidate for the first time in 1856, the explorer John C. Fremont. The platform, though, was strictly about federal territories and the issue of slavery expansion. Yet even though the party was just two years old, Republicans nearly won the election, with Democrats only getting 45 percent of the vote. Two years later, in a fusion with other factions, they elected the US Speaker of the House. The South was beginning to see the political handwriting on the wall.

By 1860 the Republican Party took on a whole new appearance with the addition of vast economic proposals, essentially the old program of Hamilton and Henry Clay's American System. The nominee for 1860 was not some erratic adventurer but a serious politician who was himself an economic animal - Abraham Lincoln of Illinois, who referred to himself as a "Henry Clay Tariff Whig."

Lincoln was, in fact, a Hamiltonian, who believed in the merits of big government but most particularly in the area of economics. According to Gabor S. Boritt, in his book *Lincoln and the Economics of the American Dream*, if you examine Lincoln's career before the war, well more than half of everything he wrote or said was on the subject of economics - protective tariffs, national bank, fiat currency, and federal funding for internal improvements, most particularly railroad construction. Lincoln always considered himself a Whig - Boritt and David Herbert Donald call him the "Whig in the White House" - and sought to put the plan of his "beau ideal of a statesman," Henry Clay, into policy.

Such a plan was greatly concerning to the Jeffersonian South, realizing that the high tariff was designed to enrich the North, deplete the South, and reward well-connected cronies such as railroad magnates and other corporate hacks, who would also gain federal funding for internal improvements that would also benefit the North, while the bank would fund it and be perhaps as crooked and corrupt as it had been under Nicholas Biddle. In short, the new Lincoln government, based exclusively on Hamiltonian principles, would, most assuredly, intervene in the internal affairs of the Southern States and plunder them like never before. As Jerry C. Brewer has written in *Dismantling the Republic*, Northern interests were at work to turn the Jeffersonian republic into a "Consolidated Mercantile Empire."

Lincoln and his philosophy were also dangerous in another regard. He claimed to hold the Declaration of Independence in the highest regard, once referring to the American Revolution as "a struggle for national independence by a single people." His inference was that a "single people," whom he considered Northerners and Southerners to be, could not legally break up. He denied the right of any state to secede from the Union. As he said in his first inaugural address,

> Physically speaking, we cannot separate. We cannot remove our respective sections from each other nor build an impassable wall between them. A husband and wife may be divorced and go out of the presence and beyond the reach of each other; but the different parts of our country cannot do this.

Of this Jefferson Davis said,

> The monstrous conception of the creation of a new people, invested with the whole or a great part of the sovereignty which had previously belonged to the people of each state, has not a syllable to sustain it in the Constitution.

So by November 1860, it was apparent to many Southerners, particularly after the horrors of John Brown's raid the year before, that the country was about to undergo sweeping change, or a transformation, if you will, with Lincoln and this new party that was completely sectional in its nature, a party that was concerned only with Northern opinion, principles, ideals, and policies, most specifically economic.

In 1861, Southerners, completely exacerbated by the threats of the North, determined to create a government of their own, one reflecting their principles, and they believed that they had every right to do so, as believers of the right of self-determination of peoples, the very heart of the Declaration of Independence.

The contrast then between the Southern and Northern governments was vast. As the *London Times* opined on May 7, 1861, "The South wants independence, the North wants empire." Lincoln, and most Presidents after him, being of the Hamiltonian mode of thinking, established all the central tenants of Hamilton's political thought: a national banking system, a fiat currency, high protective tariffs, an income tax, money for corporations, and the suppression of civil liberties.

The Confederacy, as a government under Jefferson Davis, was administered on Jeffersonian principles, the polar opposite of Lincoln's administration. The Confederate Constitution was a culmination of Jeffersonian political thought. It was much like the U.S. Constitution, because Southerners believed that was their birthright, but it did contain numerous important changes, which only made it more Jeffersonian.

One key difference can be found in the Confederate Constitution's Article 1, Section 2, Clause 5, which gave the state legislatures the power to impeach and remove "any judicial or other Federal officer, resident and acting solely within the limits of any State." This was the heart and soul of Confederate governing principles. If federal officials meddled in state and local affairs, they could be banished from the state. This was one of the crucial components of Jeffersonian political thought, designed solely to preserve federalism. Yet establishment historians say it wasn't about states' rights.

There were also other notable differences in the Confederate Constitution that fall along Jeffersonian lines: God was mentioned in the Preamble. The President could serve only one six-year term and had a line item veto to control spending. It outlawed protective tariffs, banned the international slave trade, removed the "general welfare" clause, prohibited federally-funded internal improvements (today known as "earmarks"), required a two-thirds vote of each house of Congress for appropriations, forbid recess appointments, and prohibited persons of foreign birth who had not obtained citizenship from voting for any office on the state or federal level. All of these provisions upheld the Jeffersonian ideal.

Now consider an important question: Was this movement for Southern self-government an act of revolution? Some scholars have said it was. One definition of "revolution" reads: "a forcible overthrow of a government or social order in favor of a new system." Does that sound like something the South had done? Or does it sound more like what Lincoln did? The answer should be obvious.

The South's stand was no more a revolution than what America's fathers had done in 1776. But there's little question that Lincoln's illegal invasion and conquest of the South was a revolutionary act. The South understood and saw very clearly what Lincoln and the Republicans were up to, seceded in order to save and preserve the Jeffersonian ideal, and govern themselves, just as Americans had done 85 years before; Lincoln invaded, not to overthrow slavery, but to conquer the South, end Jeffersonian governance, and fasten on the nation his nationalistic economic policies, in precisely the same stance as the former Mother Country. As he said in his famous 1862 letter to Horace Greeley, "The sooner the national authority can be restored; the nearer the Union will be 'the Union as it was.'" His meaning was clear: to restore the "national authority" over the States.

James Henley Thornwell wrote of these issues in the midst of the war, in a book entitled *Our Danger and Our Duty,* published in 1862:

> The consequences of success on our part will be very different from the consequences of success on the part of the North. If they prevail, the whole character of the Government will be changed, and instead of a federal republic, the common agent of sovereign and independent States, we shall have a central despotism, with the notion of States forever abolished, deriving its powers from the will, and shaping its policy according to the wishes, of a numerical majority of the people; we shall have, in other words, a supreme, irresponsible democracy.
>
> On the other hand, we are struggling for constitutional freedom. We are upholding the great principles which our fathers bequeathed us, and if we should succeed, and become, as we shall, the dominant nation of this continent, we shall perpetuate and diffuse the very liberty for which Washington bled, and which the heroes of the Revolution achieved. We are not revolutionists - we are resisting revolution. We are upholding the true doctrines of the Federal Constitution. We are conservative. Our success is the triumph of all that has been considered established in the past.

Thornwell was not only correct but also eerily prophetic, for that's exactly what the South was fighting for and the North hoped to prevent.

Others saw this as well. Just consider the fact that by 1860, there were four ex-Presidents - Tyler, Van Buren, Fillmore, Pierce - still alive and another soon-to-be in James Buchanan, yet all five opposed Lincoln's election - and actively worked to derail him - and his revolution, even though four of the five were Northerners. They understood what was happening to the country.

And a revolution is exactly what we had. The Governor of Lincoln's home state of Illinois, Richard Yates, wrote in 1865, "The war has tended, more than any other event in the history of the country, to militate against the Jeffersonian idea, that 'the best government is that which governs least.' The war has not only, of necessity, given more power to, but has led to a more intimate prevision of the government over every material interest of society." This last point was one of Hamilton's, and Lincoln's, main goals.

When Confederate General Richard Taylor, son of former President Zachary Taylor, returned home to his Louisiana plantation in 1865, he found that "society has been completely changed by the war. The [French] revolution of '89 did not produce a greater change in the *Ancien régime* than has this in our social life."

Historians, even those who lived through the conflict, understood the profound changes the war brought. George Ticknor wrote in 1869 that the war had left a "great gulf between what happened before it in our century and what has happened since, or what is likely to happen thereafter. It does not seem to me as if I were living in the country in which I was born." In short, Lincoln's revolution destroyed the Age of Jefferson.

Modern scholars have also made note of this fact. As the Lincoln cult member James M. McPherson points out in *Abraham Lincoln and the Second American Revolution,*

> after the war the old decentralized federal republic became a new national polity that taxed the people directly, created an internal revenue bureau to collect these taxes, expanded the jurisdiction of federal courts, established a national currency and a national banking structure. The United States went to war in 1861 to preserve the Union; it emerged from war in 1865 having created a nation. Before 1861 the two words "United States" were generally used as a plural noun: "The United States are a republic." After 1865 the United States became a singular noun. The loose union of states became a nation.

Lincoln and his party, writes historian Heather Cox Richardson, "transformed the United States." Before the war the "national government did little more than deliver the mail, collect tariffs, and oversee foreign affairs. By the time of Appomattox, the United States had changed." Wartime Republicans constructed "a newly active national government designed to promote" a worldview of an industrialized America, with Washington playing an increasingly interventionist role.

> A strong central government dominated the postwar nation. It boasted a military of over a million men; it carried a national debt of over $2.5 billion; and it collected an array of new internal taxes, provided a national currency, distributed public lands, chartered corporations, and enforced the freedom of former slaves within state borders.

Each of these developments flew in the face of the Jeffersonian tradition. And as a result, the United States essentially lost its constitutional republic during this War of Northern Aggression and the later period of Reconstruction.

What had happened was nothing short of a crime. In fact, Henry Clay Dean of Pennsylvania, a Methodist Episcopal Preacher and Copperhead, who was featured in Mark Twain's book, *Life on the Mississippi,* authored an 1869 book with that theme in mind, entitled *The Crimes of the Civil War*. He dedicated the book to four different groups of people, descriptions that sound much like a revolution:

The first group was people like him, Northerners who had resisted:

> To the brave men, who, unmoved by the violence of party; unseduced by the temptations of wealth, and unawed by the cruelty of war, defended the priceless treasures of Constitutional Liberty; endured banishment, tortures, and death, rather than surrender their birthright, transmitted by the Fathers of 1776.

The second group was decent Union soldiers:

> To those upright soldiers, who, through, five years of carnage, corruption, plunder, rapine, and desolation, preserved their hands unstained with innocent blood, their souls unpolluted with plunder, and maintained their manhood inviolate.

The third group was working people of the North:

> To the laboring poor, whose subsistence is devoured by the combinations of Monopoly, Bankruptcy, Usury, Extortion, Standing Armies, Tax-gatherers and Usurpation.

The fourth group was Confederate soldiers:

> To the immortal dead, who surrendered their lives in defense of the honor and safety of their homes,

> and poured out their blood in rich libations to the God of Liberty.

But unfortunately the North's crimes did not end with the war but continued on during the twelve years of Reconstruction. Brownson wrote of the attitudes prevailing in his section of the country during that period.

> We have some madmen amongst us who talk of exterminating the Southern leaders, and of New Englandizing the South. We wish to see the free-labor system substituted for the slave-labor system, but beyond that we have no wish to exchange or modify Southern society, and would rather approach Northern society to it, than it to Northern society.

Reconstruction, like the war before it, continued the goal of destroying the old Jeffersonian Union and erecting a new one in its place, one based on federal government control rather than on states' rights and individual liberty. Many of the Radical Republicans, the "madmen" referred to by Brownson, like Thaddeus Stevens, sought to ethnically-cleanse the former Confederacy during Reconstruction, viewing the South as conquered territory to be treated as such. Senator Zachariah Chandler of Michigan said it this way: "A rebel has sacrificed all his rights. He has no right to life, liberty, property, or the pursuit of happiness. Everything you give him, even life itself, is a boon which he has forfeited." Stevens said the South should "be laid waste, and made a desert," then "re-peopled by a band of freemen."

Radical Republicans hated the South and Southern institutions, particularly the Jeffersonian philosophy of government, which they hoped to destroy for good. They wanted the complete subjugation of the region, vindictive punishment of the rebels, the overthrow of all Southern state governments, and the confiscation of all land and homes. Peoples from the North and West would then be sent to the South to repopulate it, ensuring that it would remain firmly Republican and solidly Lincolnian. In other words, they wanted to make the South like the North, just like Brownson had said, sweeping away all vestiges of Southern culture and politics. Such thoughts are certainly revolutionary. Lincoln's Navy Secretary, Gideon Welles, the lone conservative Democrat in the Cabinet, called the Radical plan "an atrocious scheme of plunder and robbery."

Thankfully the radical viewpoint did not prevail. Although it seemed as though the war and Radical Reconstruction killed Jeffersonianism completely, it did receive a brief revival under Grover Cleveland, a Northern proponent of Jefferson's ideas. Cleveland saw himself as in the mold of the nation's founders, especially Jefferson, who could reverse the destruction of political institutions the war and Reconstruction had wrought, just as the Sage of Monticello turned back the destructive Federalist tide in 1800. This is why the Lincolnians of his day fought so hard against his election as President, for Cleveland stands out as the lone Jeffersonian among all Presidents from Lincoln to Obama, a statesman who held as tight to those principles as any President in American history.

First elected in 1884, after twenty-four consecutive years of Lincolnian White House rule, Cleveland became the first Jeffersonian to serve as President since before the war. A quarter century of corruption, profligate spending, high taxes, and ever-expanding government had been the norm. When Cleveland entered office, he instituted honest government, ended presidential luxury, slashed the bureaucracy, halted out-of-control spending by vetoing a record 414 bills, protected the massive budget surplus that Republicans were all too eager to spend, and reduced the national debt by 20 percent. Not a bad record for a first term.

In 1888, he was defeated for a second consecutive term by Benjamin Harrison, although he won the popular vote. Though determined not to seek another term, he quickly changed his mind when he saw what the Lincolnians under President Harrison were doing to the country, and what some were doing within his beloved Jeffersonian Democratic Party, moving it closer to the Party of Lincoln in the hopes of being more successful in future elections. In 1892, Cleveland threw his hat back in the presidential ring and, like Jefferson in 1800, took back the White House and led his party to a sweep of both houses of Congress, the first time Jeffersonians controlled the entire government since 1858 under James Buchanan. The future seemed bright indeed.

Yet, sadly, fate intervened. During his second term, from 1893 to 1897, Cleveland faced a severe economic depression, one that had resulted from the massive re-imposition of Lincolnian fiscal policies during the preceding Harrison Administration. A month before Cleveland took his second oath of office, the economy began to crumble. And even though neither he nor his party had anything to do with the collapse, and even though he used Jeffersonian methods to end it within two years, Cleveland and the Democrats received all the blame. In the mid-term election in 1894 Democrats were routed, losing both houses of Congress, and in 1896, the Lincolnians were back in charge with the election of William McKinley.

In my view, the Panic of 1893 killed Jeffersonian Conservatism, as Republicans successfully spun it as a "Democratic Depression," which seemed plausible when prosperity returned under McKinley. To get around that label, Democrats began shedding Jeffersonian principles and began embracing more Lincolnian ideas, beginning with William Jennings Bryan in 1896.

But consider a few of the policy proposals that came about during the Gilded Age, which many consider a time of laissez faire conservatism: A peacetime income tax that was crafted for the express purpose of re-distributing the nation's wealth but, after passage, was killed by the Supreme Court; another wealth redistribution scheme that called for a cap on inheritance at $500,000 and all fortunes above that level would be confiscated by the government and distributed to those less fortunate; a New Deal-style public works program that would have spent $500 million to combat the Panic of 1893. Those ideas were out there and the Democratic Party began to embrace them.

By the early 20th century, one disgruntled Jeffersonian Democrat wrote that the old party "as we knew it, is dead."

As the columnist George Will has written, "We honor Jefferson, but live in Hamilton's country." But in reality we live in Lincoln's country.

Our political heritage of Jeffersonian values seems as if it died with Grover Cleveland because it has never been resurrected in a major political party. It only seems to be alive in the hearts of true Sons of Jefferson and true Sons of the South. As Senator Willie P. Mangum of North Carolina wrote, it is Southerners that were "the real conservators of our political system." And even though radicals today are working to destroy our heritage, as John F. Kennedy once said, "A man may die, nations may rise and fall, but an idea lives on." Indeed, ideas are bulletproof.

THE SOUTH AND AMERICA'S WARS FOR RIGHTEOUSNESS

RICHARD GAMBLE

IN 1874, A YOUNG WOODROW Wilson, or Tommy Wilson, if you can imagine it, as he was still known to friends and family, left Davidson College in NC after his freshman year to recuperate from an illness. He came here to Wilmington, his father pastored Wilmington's first Presbyterian Church over on the corner of 3rd and Orange. According to Josephus Daniels, President Wilson's Secretary of the Navy from 1913-1921, and himself a North Carolinian, the adolescent Wilson "talked to sailors on the waterfront, played shortstop on the neighborhood baseball team, and swam in the Cape Fear at the foot of Dock Street." Secretary Daniels also reports that Tommy was the first person in North Carolina to own a bicycle and startled local residents by riding his contraption around the streets of Wilmington. Daniels admits that Wilson was something of a social misfit.

The Secretary of the Navy continues his account: "The river and the ships fascinated the youth. Their color and associations of adventure and romance fed his imagination. The lure of the sea was strong upon him and it was in those days that he had his heart set on going to the naval Academy. His father saw that he was meant for letters and teachers and politics and set his foot down upon a naval career. When the Navy lost Tommy Wilson as a future admiral, it gained in 1913 a commander in chief whose marvelous grasp of naval matters made him the real leader of the men who go down to the seas in ships."

Jumping ahead 40 years to the autumn of 1915, Wilson was now the commander in Chief of the Army and Navy, and Josephus

Daniels' boss. The First World War had been underway in Europe for a little over a year. Its brutal slaughter would intensify shortly on the fields of Verdun and the Somme, and it would last another three years. Grimm realities unknown to anyone at the time, but certain to make the world of 1918 utterly unlike the world of 1914. American intervention on the side of the Allied Powers had not yet happened in 1915. And it is important not to see the next steps as inevitable. The future at this moment is filled with potential. History could have followed another trajectory with consequences we could only speculate about for America and the world. Woodrow Wilson had called for neutrality at the war's beginning. Few citizens, a year later, thought America would enter a war so far from home. War with Mexico seemed more probable. But some ambitious people did envision a remarkably aggressive, redemptive, universal mission for the United States

Listen to what one publication had to say about the ideal American citizen and his role in the world at that moment in 1915:

> The imperialism of the American is a duty and credit to humanity. He is the highest type of imperial master, he makes beautiful the land he touches. Beautiful with moral and physical cleanliness. There should be no doubt that even with all possible moral refinement, it is the absolute right of the nation to live to its full intensity, to expand, to found colonies, to get richer and richer by any proper means, such as armed conquest, commerce, diplomacy... Such expansion as an aim is an inalienable right, and in the case of the United States it is a particular duty because we are idealists, and thereby bound by establishing protectorate over the weak, to protect them from unmoral Kultur.

Now that word, "Kultur," referred to Germany and its imperial ambitions. Clearly, some Americans had already made up their minds one year into the war that the United States had a major role to play in world affairs and that the principal obstacle to those ambitions was Germany. But notice that American colonialism would be unlike Germany's, it would be "beautiful" and "moral" and "benevolent." These extraordinary words about America's righteous imperialism came from an anonymous writer for *Seven Seas Magazine*, in its November 1915 issue. This journal was the short-lived mouthpiece from the Navy League, an organization founded in 1902 during Teddy Roosevelt's administration, on the model of similar organizations in Britain and Germany. Its purpose was to promote construction of an offensive modern naval fleet second to none. It still exists, it boasts 50,000 members and lobbies congress for large defense expenditures.

Mobilized by the coming of war in 1914, and then by Germany's sinking of the Lusitania in May 1915, the Navy League called for a dramatic built up of armaments, seeking a half billion dollars in new spending, back when half a billion dollars was a lot of money and did more than service a few minutes of debt. The Navy League's members included a number of high profile leaders from industry, Wall Street, politics, and religion. With executives from steel and other heavy industries that would profit handsomely from increased naval appropriations, it is hard to avoid the conclusion that this organization's purposes were pretty transparent. Its backers stood to gain much.

The *Seven Seas* article was quotable, to say the least, and it stirred up a furor of responses - ranging from the pacifist Henry Ford, to prominent Socialists, to an assortment of liberal clergymen allied with the federal council of churches. Ford took out large advertisements in such periodicals as *Successful Farming*, to sound the alarm at America's Heartland. Arranging saber-rattling, patriotic organizations like the Navy League on one side, and political and religious pacifists on the other, it would be easy to frame the story of America's division over war preparedness and intervention from 1914-1917 as a simple story of interventionists vs. isolationists, of conservatives vs. liberals, of right wing vs. left wing. But these artificial categories don't work and only mask a more complex and interesting reality.

In the 1930's, Dorothy Parker, famously commented that actress Katharine Hepburn's performance ran the gamut of emotions from "A to B." I think of this witticism every time I encounter historians who offer narrow accounts of the past that masquerade as the whole story; who offer false choices that pretend to be the whole range of opinion and available options for policy makers. These historians and journalists and politicians and television celebrities focus our attention narrowly on a spectrum of judgments ranging only from A to B, and leave us with the impression that we have the whole story from A-Z.

Telling the story of the debate over American preparedness and subsequent intervention in the First World War, only through the framework of artificial categories...if we do that, we miss great swathes of historical reality. I have taken this digression to prepare the way for another reaction to the ambition of the Navy League and kindred spirits. A reaction to military preparedness and intervention that we shouldn't allow to remain invisible. To help fill in those gaps in our collective memory I offer you a sketch this morning of the resistance to Woodrow Wilson's foreign policy from two southerners: the North Carolinian Claude Kitchin, and the Georgian Tom Watson.

I cannot offer now a generalized description of THE South's response to intervention in 1917. It varied tremendously among Southern politicians, clergymen, bankers, lawyers, and small town newspaper editors. For every Southern senator willing to defy the president and vote against the war resolution, there were several who backed him and his policies. For every southern House member who voted against the war resolution, there were several who voted for it. And more than a few Southern congressmen could spout Wilsonian platitudes with the best of them. But a simple tally of up and down votes among Southern senators and congressman reveals less than it might appear to. And it's possible that the fact that the South ended up fighting in WWI matters less than how they thought and spoke about the war. About America's traditions and her place in the world. I think a parallel would be Nathaniel Macon, who voted for the war of 1812, but his reasonings about the war matter a lot. It is obvious that the South was not pacifist in 1917, but it is also obvious that it was not militarist or imperialist, either.

Before I proceed to these two men. I need to make one more digression to explain the title of my talk. What is a War for Righteousness? I have borrowed this phrase in the past and again today from the Cambridge historian, Herbert Butterfield. His concept of a war for righteousness is the most helpful way to think about one important tendency in American thought that helped justify US intervention in the First World War. A troubling tendency, that Claude Kitchin and Tom Watson resisted, even if with little success.

Butterfield argued in a short essay, entitled the "War for Righteousness," published in the 1950s that the massive destruction, loss of life and duration of the First World War were attributable, not to modern technology and industrialized warfare alone, the war's destructiveness required an act of will to use those perfected means of mass slaughter against the enemy. The scale and intensity of that war had at least as much to do with the decision on all sides to wage a war of ideas. An unlimited war, for unlimited means, for unlimited ends, a revival, he feared, of the zeal of the 16th century wars of religion that brought so much suffering to Europe after the Reformation. Significantly, Butterfield pointed to the American Civil War as the first reappearance of that righteous zeal. A war to impose an idea, or to borrow Edmund Burke's description of the French Jacobins, a war waged with an armed doctrine. The First World War became such a war for Righteousness. An ideological crusade, and many Americans embraced that formula for how they themselves pictured their enemy, and the meaning of the war. They followed President Wilson into a 20th century crusade - a word that he used more than once.

Recall what the *Seven Seas Magazine* claimed back in 1915: "We are idealists." What kind of a war will you end up fighting if you combine a self-righteous, redemptive, universal mission with a world class navy and army? What did a couple of non-interventionists in the South make all of this? And what can we learn from them? And while I'm asking questions, let me lay out what I think the real questions were from 1914-1917. That is from the outbreak of the war in Europe until America's intervention.

Was the United States adequately armed? If so, for what end was it adequately armed? For its own defense? That would be one thing. For intervention? That would be another. Or maybe for empire? That would be something else entirely. But there are further questions.

Just what exactly was the policy objective? Who has the constitutional responsibility to formulate that policy? Who should judge its merits? And how should it all be paid for? The debate in Washington and within the Democratic party that was in power in 1915 was not between the nation being unarmed or armed, vulnerable or safe. Whatever the impression left at the time and since, the debate was not between pacifists and militarists. The press might spin it that way, but these were false choices, and they remain false choices.

Congressman Claude Kitchin saw that very article in *Seven Seas Magazine*, and he was not a fan. He was a North Carolina native from near Scotland Neck, about parallel with Kitty Hawk and not too far from Nathaniel Macon's home. An agrarian traditionalist and enemy of Henry Grady's industrialized new South, Kitchin held the 2nd district House seat for over twenty years, from 1901 until his death in 1923. He served as speaker of the House from 1915 until the Republican midterm victories in 1918 cost the Democrats control of the House. He also chaired the powerful House Ways and Means committee, and sat as a prominent and well informed member of the Naval Affairs committee. In short, Kitchin was a formidable and respected politician who respected his party and the Wilson administration when he could, but was nobody's lap dog.

Up to 1915, President Wilson had publicly opposed the naval armament recommendation coming from the government's own naval board. He and Kitchin agreed on this, but Wilson got behind the armaments push in the summer of 1915, and Kitchin's letters show that he clearly suspected Wilson of intending to enter the war as early as 1915. In an important speech in New York City on November 4, 1915, President Wilson announced the scale of the proposed build up. Including the Navy armaments and a 400,000 man citizen army, which he called the "Continental Army," that would be ready to mobilize on short notice.

According to his biographer, Arthur Link, the naval legislation would, in the first five years, augment the Navy by "10 battleships, 6 battle cruisers, 10 cruisers, 50 destroyers, 100 submarines and lesser craft" at a cost of $500,000,000 dollars. This plan, if implemented, would put the U.S. on a trajectory to reach parity with Great Britain, mistress of the world's largest Navy, within 10 years. Kitchin met with Wilson, as you might expect as House leader four days later to discuss the legislation. He and the president disagreed profoundly, but both publicly said that the vote on this proposal was a matter of individual conscience and not a party matter.

But given Kitchin's rank as Democratic speaker of the House, it is hard to imagine that politics didn't figure somewhere in their conversation. Wilson could not have been pleased. In a statement given to the press on November 20th, speaker Kitchin quoted loosely from the same paragraph in the *Seven Seas Magazine* article that I read earlier. He pointed out a few salient facts: The United States was already large, growing, and modernizing under existing legislation. Kitchin argued at length that the Navy and coastal batteries were adequate for defense. More than that and the object must be something other than the protection of the United States. It must be, he reasoned, to intervene in Europe or to build an empire of our own. He accused the Navy League and its magazine of stimulating the public's appetite for "big militarism and navalism." He called the program big, enormous, revolutionary. In January and early February 1916, Wilson toured the Midwest to campaign for the legislation, and returned to the White House confident that public opinion would swap any opposition in Congress. But Kitchin wrote to his friend, William Jennings Bryan: "I see no real change in the attitudes of the members since the president's western tour."

Kitchin was probably right, but events in the legislative process and the political process would soon overtake him. Joining forces, the president and Republicans in the Senate and House managed in mid-August to pass the largest naval armaments bill in U.S. history, or in history period, Secretary Daniels boasted. They did so by a wide margin in the House of 283 to 51, with 35 Democrats voting no out of those 51 no's. With the exception of one congressman from Pennsylvania, all the no votes came from the Midwest and the South. The New York Times noted Kitchin's frustration with the administration for changing course so abruptly. He complained, the paper reported, that Wilson "expects me today to eat my words uttered when I opposed such a program as originally offered in this House by the Republican minority. Approval of this building program means that the United States today becomes the most militaristic naval nation on earth." The larger story of Claude Kitchin and his often lonely fight against the Wilson administration and the metropolitan newspapers would take us into matters of how the expanded Navy and army would be paid for, and later into the struggle over the conscription law, which incidentally, more congressman voted against than voted against the declaration of war.

The only book on Claude Kitchin I can point you to is Alex Arnett's 1937 volume: *Claude Kitchin and the Wilson War Policies*. Arnett's book received mostly positive reviews from his peers, at a time when the memory of the war and of the political controversy surrounding it was still fresh. Arnett's book joined a substantial and growing list of so called "Revisionist Histories" in the 1920s and 30s that, in the words of one reviewer, argued that the entrance of the United States into the World War was a tragic mistake.

But we need to turn quickly to the spring of 1917 and the declaration of war. President Wilson delivered his war message on Monday evening, April 2. The Senate debated and voted for war by an overwhelming margin on April 4, a vote of 82-6. The House debated throughout the week and into the early hours of Friday, April 6 - Good Friday, as it happens. A tempting symbol that congressman eager to fight a redemptive war just couldn't resist mentioning. Kitchin spoke around midnight April 5 - April 6. He voted against the resolution for war, one of only 50 in the House to do so. But he retained his position as majority leader right through the war. Despite the predictions of the press. Kitchin began his speech before his colleagues by rebuking those who suggested that the impending vote on the war resolution would mark the difference between patriot and coward.

"It takes neither moral nor physical courage to declare a war for others to fight," he said. "Moreover, it is evidence of neither loyalty nor patriotism for one to urge others to get into a war when he knows that he himself is going to keep out." Kitchin affirmed that in voting against the war measure, his conscience was clear and his action would be a legacy his descendants would be proud of. "I cannot leave my children lands and riches. I cannot leave them fame. But I can leave them the name of an ancestor who, mattering not the consequences to himself, never dared to do his duty as God gave him to see it."

Kitchin then called America the last hope of peace on Earth, goodwill toward men, and the only remaining star of hope for Christendom. That might be stronger language than I would be comfortable with, but the absence here and throughout the speech of anything resembling a religious crusade is unmistakable. Especially in contrast to the extravagant claims of many of his colleagues and the president. America, in Kitchin's judgement, was the last holdout in a world gone mad. Its entry meant that the European War, already the greatest war in human history, would become a truly global war.

"Whatever be the rewards or penalties of this nation's step, I shall always believe that we could and ought to have kept out of this war." Wilson campaigned for re-election just months before on the slogan "He Kept Us Out of War." Kitchin once boasted, "We kept him out of war." But the speaker knew this was no longer possible. Nevertheless, at this late hour, he still tried to remind his colleagues and the nation that there was enough guilt to go around among the Allied and Central Powers. Despite the simple story

America might be telling itself at that moment, the war could not be understood as a contest between light and dark, the righteous and the damned, Christ and Antichrist. Kitchin recounted the history of Britain's violations of American neutrality since the beginning of the war. In fact, Britain's conduct seems so similar to Germany's that the U.S. had as much reason to go to war with one as the other. America could continue a policy of armed neutrality, a strategy Kitchin had voted for in support of the president a month earlier. It could do so without sacrificing its honor, safety, or interest.

Here's one paragraph to sum up Kitchin's objections best:

> The House and the country should thoroughly understand that we are asked to declare war, not to protect alone American lives and American rights on the high seas, we are to make the cause of Great Britain, France, and Russia - right or wrong - our cause. We are to make their quarrel - right or wrong - our quarrel. We are to fight out, with all the resources in men, money, and credit of the government and its people - a difference between the belligerence of Europe to which we were and are utter strangers. Nothing in that cause, nothing in that quarrel has or does involve a moral or equitable or material interest in, or obligation of, our government or our people.

At this point, the House speaker promised to give his full support to the war effort, should the Constitutional process of deliberation by the people's representatives result in a declaration of war that night - and he kept his word. From that moment, Kitchin led the House as it debated war mobilization measures, ranging from the contentious issue of the draft to heated debates over taxes to pay for the war. He might continue to disagree with the administration over how to pay for the war, but he ruined his own health working to assure American victory once the "final word," as he called it, had been spoken.

The memory of Claude Kitchin's courageous stance in 1917 seemed to stamp his reputation from that moment forward. One after another of the memorial addresses given in the House after his death in 1923 mentions that dramatic night. And the word "courage" appears as a constant refrain. Republican representative William Green of Iowa, who voted for the war, said of his colleague:

> I never knew a man who had more courage, and I remember quite well, as many of you do who are now before me, the time he stood here when we declared war against Germany. It was a most fateful decision that he was making. An overwhelming majority, not only of his own side of the House but of my own side, was against him. Public opinion was aroused, and the disposition was to treat everyone who did not support the declaration as one who was almost a traitor to his country. Truly, he was compelled to walk the path almost alone, and many felt that he himself must have feared that he had taken a course which would lead to his political ruin. But no matter how much we might have disagreed with him at that time with reference to the vote that was to be cast, every man that listened to him knew that Claude Kitchin was absolutely sincere in his convictions and directed by them alone in the action which he took.

In the 1870s, we left Woodrow Wilson cycling around the streets of Wilmington. By the early 1880s, he had graduated from Princeton, had passed his bar exam in Georgia, and was now practicing law in Atlanta in the new South. The Civil War was a recent memory and former confederate Alexander H. Stephens was Georgia's governor. Unknown to Wilson, a young state representative named Thomas E. Watson walked past his law offices on Marietta Street every day on the way to the state house.

Tom Watson was born near Thompson Georgia in 1856, the same year as Woodrow Wilson and about a decade before Claude Kitchin. He practiced law in Thompson, beginning in 1877, served in the Georgia House in 1882, was elected to one term in the U.S. House in 1890, ran for Vice President on the Populist party ticket in 1896, and then as the Populist candidate for president in 1904 and 1908. In 1908, he won election to the U.S. Senate from Georgia and held that office until his death in 1922. As author and editor, he wrote biographies of Thomas Jefferson, Andrew Jackson, and Napoleon and a two volume history of France, and he edited *The Jeffersonian* and *Watson's Magazine*. Regrettably, little serious scholarship has been devoted to Watson. One biography appeared in the 1920s with utterly inadequate treatment of Watson's reaction to the First World War, and in 1938 C. Vann Woodward published his biography.

The Library of the University of North Carolina has digitized the archives of the entire Watson collection of correspondence, photographs, issues of his magazine, even silent film footage of Watson at home. There is a wealth of material and no excuse for him not being better known.

No word is really too strong to capture Watson's abiding animosity towards Woodrow Wilson. He loathed him. He loathed him in his various incarnations as historian, Ivy League educator, reformer, presidential candidate, and president. Wilson provoked Watson as early as 1903, when Wilson was early in his tenure as president of Princeton, and known as the author of a five volume history of the American people. It irked Watson that a man born in Virginia and tied to South Carolina, North Carolina, and Georgia could display such partiality for New England and slight the South's contributions to American history. Watson chastised Wilson by name no fewer than eight times in the text and footnotes of his biography of Thomas Jefferson. In 1905, he called Wilson "an insufferable, impractical prig" for his proposal to moralize the big business trusts. When Wilson ran for the Democratic nomination in 1912, Watson campaigned for his Democratic challenger, Oscar Underwood, instead and said he could never vote for Wilson. True to his word, he actually backed Teddy Roosevelt's Bull Moose progressive party in the three way race that year in 1912, against the incumbent Taft. A strategy resorted to by several Southern newspaper editors, who couldn't hold their noses long enough to vote for Wilson. One South Carolina editor called him a "climatized Yankee."

When the First World War broke out, Watson wielded his editorials against the preparedness campaign, militarism, intervention, the draft, and the espionage and sedition acts of 1917. His relentless assaults on the administration led the attorney general and the postmaster general to shut down *The Jeffersonian* by denying it the use of the mails under the conditions of the espionage act. The terms of which could have meant prosecution for Watson and jail time in the federal prison in Atlanta. Just picture this, where he would have joined an odd assortment of socialists, Jehovah's Witnesses, German orchestra conductors and musicians, and fellow newspaper editors. Stopped at the post office in Savannah for opposing the draft law, *The Jeffersonian* suspended publication in the summer of 1917. And living as we do in a world of Wikileaks, it is hard to imagine a time when a president and a cabinet could impose censorship so effectively. *The Jeffersonian,* or simply "The Jeff" as its subscribers called it, at turns angry, sarcastic, clever, or a bit crude, but always barreling ahead at full throttle, fumed over massive loans to the allies, the rapid consolidation of war time power in Washington, the breakdown of Constitutional limits and strict construction, and the indignity of conscription. Watson's historical memory went all the way back to the War of 1812 and he quoted often from opposition to the draft then by Daniel Webster and others. To emphasize how revolutionary he thought Wilson was, Tom Watson said nice things about Daniel Webster and Grover Cleveland, and even pointed out that Abraham Lincoln had resorted to conscription, suspension of habeas corpus, and emancipation as emergency war measures. Wilson, Watson charged, was under no such urgent compulsion to defend America in 1917.

Critics of the South will challenge the sincerity of Watson's principles by saying they were anything but principles, and merely a cover for entrenched racism and a desperate attempt to deny the federal government any increased power, lest it wield that power to interfere with race relations in the South. But it strikes me as unfaithful to the record of the past to dismiss Watson's principles as anything more than rhetorical fancy dress to cover up a cranky populism that couldn't make its peace with modernity, progress, and America's world role. It's difficult to sort through all this, and Watson presents a unique challenge. How do we defend Watson's Constitutionalism when he seems so vulnerable to attack? And if we use his arguments, do we make our own challenges vulnerable? Watson's wartime strategy was to hammer away in editorials in "The Jeff" at the violations of such founding principles as delegated and enumerated powers, limited government, and civil liberties. He charted the growth of the Leviathan state through the crises of The Civil War, The Spanish American War, and now the Great War.

"If Germany posed an imminent threat to the United States," he asked, "why did the United States have to cross 3,000 miles of ocean to engage the enemy?" And he made it clear that he was not a pacifist: "I am not too proud to fight", as the president said he was.

"But I am too conservative to leave the new world and go hunting for a fight in the old world."

Here is an example of Watson's strategy. In one issue of "The Jeff," he reacted to Wilson's May 30, 1917 speech at Arlington National Cemetery:

> In the providence of God, America will have an opportunity to show that she was born to serve mankind? We are saying to all mankind that we did not set this government up in order that we might have a selfish and separate liberty, we are now ready to come to your assistance and fight out upon the fields of the world the cause of human liberty. In this thing, America retains her full dignity and the full fruition of her great purpose.

To these claims, Tom Watson unleashed the following barrage:

> If you can filter this sentimental moonshine into something tangible and practical, you are gifted with more gray matter than God gave to me. If that sort of talk means anything at all, it means that, after we shall have rectified governmental affairs in Europe, we must next turn our quixotic attention to Asia, then to Africa, then to Oceana. And after we shall have remodeled the internal concerns of India, Persia, Turkey, Afghanistan, China, Japan, and a few other countries where conditions are not so ideal as they are in this republic, when I say we shall have finished our circuit of creation as universal redressers of national wrongs, we may at length be content to come home and stay there and attend to our own business.

This is the voice Wilson and his cabinet silenced in the summer of 1917. These were difficult years for Watson's family and his health, and although he found the strength to win a seat in the U.S. Senate in 1920 and seemed to enjoy himself immensely, he died of a stroke in 1922. One year before Claude Kitchin, and two years before Woodrow Wilson.

What can we learn from this brief and inadequate from key opposition to Woodrow Wilson and intervention? As a historian I hesitate to reduce a complex past into a set of bullet-point lessons. But Kitchin and Watson do help us ponder certain things of enduring significance to America. First, in their insistence on limited Constitutional government, we hear distinct echoes of the Anti-Federalists of the 1780s, the Kentucky and Virginia resolutions of 1798 and Jefferson's warning in his first inaugural in 1801 against entangling alliances in Europe. Second, the reaction of these Southerners to WWI helps us to understand the question of how and when America lost its fear of political power. One of the most consistent threads in Colonial America and the early Republic was the certainty that power would be accumulated and abused. The final article of Jefferson's Kentucky Resolution states "free government is founded in jealousy and not confidence. It is jealousy, and not confidence which prescribes limited constitutions to bind down those who we are obliged to trust with power..." his conclusion continues "in questions of power then, let no more be said of confidence in man, but bind him down from mischief by the chains of the Constitution."

Claude Kitchin and Tom Watson proposed to bind Wilson down from mischief by the chains of the Constitution in 1917. Thirdly, the Southern opponents of America's wars for Righteousness remind us of a stance on U.S. foreign policy that was neither pacifist, nor militarist. Neither doctrinaire isolationist, nor doctrinaire interventionist. A conservative foreign policy falls into neither of these ideological traps. Perhaps you will think of other implications we ought to draw out of the experience of 1917. If you encounter

Tommy Wilson cycling around the streets of Wilmington: stay alert, stay out of his way, and consider the legacy of American intervention in the first World War, and the neglected legacy of Southern opposition to Wars for Righteousness.

Chesty Puller and the Southern Military Tradition

Michael Martin

LEWIS BURWELL PULLER is a Marine Corps legend and American hero. Nicknamed "Chesty" for his burly physique, he was one of the most combat-hardened leaders in military history and saw action in Haiti, Nicaragua, WWII, and Korea. The winner of five Navy Crosses and many other medals, he will always be remembered as a fierce warrior and proud patriot.

One area of Chesty's life that deserves more scholarly research is his southern heritage. He was born in Virginia in 1898 and was raised on stories of the Confederacy. His grandfather, John Puller, was killed while riding under Jeb Stuart at the battle of Kelly's Ford in 1863. Local veterans told young Chesty about his grandfather's bravery, as John had stayed atop his saddle long after having his midsection torn apart by a cannon. After his grandfather's death, federals burned the Puller home and his grandmother was forced to walk ten miles, through a sleet storm, for help.

Puller was proud of his ancestry, and his southern roots ran much deeper than The War Between the States (his term of choice for the "Civil War"). His family had come to Virginia in the early 1600s and he could trace back relatives to the colony's House of Burgesses. Chesty noted that he was also a relative of Patrick Henry, George S. Patton, and that he had a great-uncle named Robert Williams, who deserted the south to join the federal army (the Virginia portion of the family stopped speaking to Williams after this, and he later went on to marry the widow of Stephen A. Douglas). Another famous cousin of Puller's, named Page

McCarthy, was a Confederate captain that fought the last legal duel in Virginia and killed his opponent.

The Confederacy and its legacy left a lasting impression on a young Chesty. As a boy, he witnessed Robert E. Lee Jr. bring a buggy by his home weekly to sell eggs and vegetables to support the Lee family. Puller's favorite Confederate was Willis Eastwood, who rode with his grandfather and became mayor of West Point. In addition, the Puller home was filled with pictures of great Confederates like Robert E. Lee and Stonewall Jackson.

As a southerner, Chesty also learned the importance of land and self-sufficiency. After his father's death in 1908, Chesty began trapping to support his family. He would capture muskrats, sell the hides for fifteen cents each and then sell the carcasses to poorer families for five cents. He also would catch local crabs and sell them for twenty five cents a dozen. By the age of twelve, young Puller had killed his first turkey and also learned how to hunt rabbits. After his military fighting career was over many years later, Chesty noted that he learned more about the art of war by hunting and trapping, than he learned from any school. He insisted that the skills he learned as a kid, living off the land, saved his life many times in combat.

Puller had spent his entire childhood admiring the military leaders of the south. In particular, he loved Stonewall Jackson and he admired the large statue of Jackson that stood at VMI, where Jackson was formerly a professor. One of Puller's most prized possessions was a copy of George Henderson's biography of Stonewall Jackson, which Chesty had read repeatedly. He underlined most of the text, wrote Jackson's famous quote "Never take counsel of your fears." The book also contained notes on the casualties of Chesty's men at Guadalcanal and his medals. It was referred to so frequently that it was embedded with dirt and held together with bicycle tape. In many ways, Lewis Puller and

Stonewall lived parallel lives. They were both proud Virginians that scored low on marks as Puller did at VMI and Jackson at West Point, yet were unmatched in the leadership on the battlefield. Chesty also frequently visited the tomb of Robert E. Lee at Washington and Lee University campus. A documentary, directed by John Ford and narrated by John Wayne, titled "Chesty: A Tribute to a Legend" features scenes of an elderly Chesty visiting the tomb of Lee.

In the tradition of many other famous southerners, Chesty also had an appreciation for the classics. At a young age, he picked up a copy of Caesar's *Gallic Wars* and even translated it from Latin. All of these experiences (living off the land, being raised on stories of the south, an interest in military leadership early on) would help mold Chesty into an ideal soldier.

Chesty exemplified the southern military tradition by having an unsurpassed sense of duty to his country, and by being a fierce warrior. The military excellence of the south can be traced back to before the American Revolution. George Washington and Francis Marion, for example, both gained their initial combat experience in the French and Indian War. It could be argued that Chesty was a more efficient leader than both of these men. Contrary to popular myth, Washington was not a great tactician or leader and his victory at Yorktown can really be attributed to the French. One of Washington's most memorable moments is enduring hardship at Valley Forge, which Chesty Puller compared to his experience in Korea by saying:

"Our forefathers at Valley Forge have been mentioned here tonight as they often are. Well, I can tell you that Valley Forge was something like a picnic compared to what your young Americans went through at the Chosin Reservoir, and they came out of it fine. It never was anything like twenty-five below zero at Valley Forge, either."

Francis Marion, known as the "Swamp Fox," used guerilla tactics and partisan warfare to fight the British in South Carolina. This type of fighting drove the British out of the Carolinas and into Virginia, where they eventually surrendered. This method of warfare today is referred to as "maneuver warfare" and has been officially adopted as the Marine Corps doctrine. Marine Corps tactics and the history of southern warfare go hand-in-hand; even today, Parris Island, South Carolina is the main training center for the Marines on the east coast and graduates at least 17,000 men and women per year.

The concept of maneuver warfare is defined by the Corps as "warfighting philosophy that seeks to shatter the enemy's cohesion through a variety of rapid, focused, and unexpected actions which create a turbulent and rapidly deteriorating situation with which the enemy cannot cope." This was exactly how Chesty was operating in Nicaragua, Haiti, Korea, and the Pacific.

Southern men like Francis Marion and Nathan Bedford Forrest also implemented these ideas of hitting the enemy hard and fast, with accurate firepower. All of the great southern military leaders, from Washington and Marion, to Lee, Jackson, and Forrest, and then finally to Chesty, were also beloved by their men. Washington got his men through Valley Forge by making sure they had a cup of rum each day and making himself visible to the troops. Francis Marion's men were unpaid and soldiered on their own accord. Forrest will always be remembered for his battle philosophy of being "first with the most." Lee and Jackson were men of unshakeable faith and inspirational leadership.

Chesty is still frequently quoted in the Marine Corps, with men carrying on his quotes like "We're surrounded? Good, now we can fire at those bastards from every direction." On another occasion, when testing a flamethrower, Puller asked "Where the hell do you put the bayonet?" so that he could stab the enemy after burning them. Puller will always be remembered for his courage and actual presence among his men. Many leaders from Puller's day were promoted on the basis of their letter-writing ability, and literally gave orders from station wagons, far from the front lines. Chesty, on the other hand, appealed to his men's senses and spiked morale by his presence. He made sure his men had good chow, shelter, and preferred taking care of matters hands on.

After the Korean War, Chesty's popularity soared. This presence, combined with his straightforward honesty, soon made him many enemies in Washington. In his early military days, Chesty was chasing bandits and collecting tributes from other countries. By the Vietnam era, Marines were being used to *pay* tributes to other countries. Chesty was not afraid to call it like he saw it and comment on the misuse of the military. He was a proud believer in *esprit de corps,* which is love for one's military machine above all else. Puller did not believe in using the military to give money to countries, especially in the case of billions we will probably never be paid back. He firmly related this belief to his understanding of southern history in a never-before transcribed 1959 speech where he stated:

"I can remember when our great president, Andrew Jackson, sent a navy ship to Italy and gave its captain orders to fire a few shots over the city, send a detail ashore, and collect what they owe us. He fired a few shots over the town, he didn't have to send the Marines ashore to go and get it. By God, they brought the money out."

Puller also commented that the military was fighting to sustain war in Vietnam, not to win. He also openly criticized the devaluation of the American dollar, the move away from the gold standard, and inflation. All of these topics were discussed in his 1959 speech, where Chesty openly lamented the upward-spiraling cost of living, combined with the devaluation of the dollar–things which he argued were causing the production of counterfeit currency. He stated that the military was also increasing its expenditures on unnecessary things like private baths for each soldier. Even with all of his dissatisfaction, he always kept his home open to Marines and continued to volunteer for service into his 60s.

Devastation struck Chesty's family after his only son, Lewis B. Puller Jr., lost both legs and parts of his hands in Vietnam. This occurred after years of Chesty's critical comments of United States policy, and resulted in Chesty's desire to offer his own ideas to make the country stronger. One solution Chesty suggested to improve the United States world-wide presence was to give less money to scientists, and put money towards putting young men in schools around the world. This would integrate young Americans into other cultures, help them truly learn languages, and give the United States an advantage in trade and communications.

When we examine Chesty through the lens of his southern heritage, his life and actions begin to make a lot more sense. His combat skills were second to none and reminiscent of men like Francis Marion, Stonewall, and Nathan Bedford Forrest. His devotion to liberty is reminiscent of men like Washington and Lee. Also like a true southerner, Chesty believed in limited government and low taxation. Puller may not have been the best public speaker or man of letters. But he was and will always be a true son of the south. His own history deserves just as much examination as his military leadership.

The Political Economy and Social Thought of Louisa S. McCord

Karen Stokes

THE NAME OF THE LADY I'm introducing today, the Southern intellectual Louisa Susannah Cheves McCord, or as she's usually called, Louisa S. McCord, is generally not known today. In the antebellum era, she was the author of numerous essays on political economy and social issues. Her other writings included poetry, reviews, and a blank verse drama entitled *Gaius Gracchus.* She also translated a book written by Frederic Bastiat, a French political economist, which was published in 1848 as *Sophisms of the Protective Policy.* Although Louisa McCord has been written about here and there in the 19th and 20th centuries, it's only relatively recently that she's begun to receive her due recognition, as one of the most significant thinkers of the antebellum South. Most importantly, in 1995 and 1996, her writings were collected and published in two volumes. The first volume contains her political and social essays, while the second offers her poetry, drama, biographical writings, and letters. Both books were edited by Richard C. Lounsbury, a classical scholar.

A two volume anthology published in 1993 entitled, *The American Intellectual Tradition* put Louisa McCord in the company of Jonathan Edwards, Thomas Jefferson, George Mason, John C. Calhoun, and other luminaries of 19th century America. The editors made the claim for her that she was the most intellectually influential female author in the Old South, and the only woman in antebellum America to write extensively about political economy and social theory. She was born in Charleston,

South Carolina, on December 3, 1810. Her Father, Langdon Cheves, an attorney and planter from Abbeville district, achieved national immanence as a statement, jurist, and financier. He was a U.S. Representative and served as Speaker of the House from 1814 until his retirement from Congress in 1815. During his tenure as speaker, one of his most important accomplishments was to defeat the rechartering of the Bank of the United States. In 1816, after Langdon Cheves had retired from Congress, the bank was rechartered, and in 1819 he accepted the urgent request from his friends to take over the bank and become its director. In doing so, Cheves gave up the opportunity to serve on the Supreme Court, for which President Monroe had appointed him.

Thanks to three years of mismanagement, the bank was in a deplorable condition, its liabilities exceeding its assets. John Quincy Adams recorded in his diary at the time that he feared a national convulsion would result from its failure. By 1822, however, Cheves' policies had succeeded in restoring its credit. In politics, Langdon Cheves was an opponent of nullification, favoring secession as the solution for state government grievances if necessary, and he was a delegate to the 1850 Nashville convention. Until the age of 10, Louisa McCord received the usual education given to girls of her social class. But when it was discovered that she had an aptitude and a passion for mathematics, her father saw to it that she received the same instruction as her brothers.

In a thesis published in 1919, Jesse M. Frazier described another dimension of Louisa's formative years. Frazier wrote:

"In her father's study and at his table, she heard the discourse of his contemporaries: Webster, Calhoun, Clay, and their associates. Political economy was the gospel of their theories, statecraft was their game. The young girl, hearing them express their theories, seeing them play their game, learned to think deeply on political issues. She noted the hearts and minds of great men at work."

Along the same lines, her cousin William Poacher Miles wrote of her: "The bent of her genius was rather for matters of state policy and political economy, rather than subjects commonly called 'general literature.'" Now was this strange when we consider the long, public life of her father, during which she was habitually thrown with the leading statesmen of the country and so often heard discussed the then absorbing topics of states' rights, free trade, tariffs, and the banks?

In 1840, Louisa McCord married David James McCord of St. Matthew's Parish. He was a prominent lawyer and an editor, the author of numerous legal works, and a state legislator, and unlike Louisa's father, a devoted advocate of the doctrine of nullification. The 15 years of Louisa's marriage to David J. McCord before his death in 1855 were the richest and busiest in terms of her writing. During this period, she was published in such journals as the *Southern Quarterly, DuBose Review, The Southern Literary Gazette,* and the *Southern Literary Messenger.* Her drama, Gaius Gracchus, a book of poetry entitled *My Dreams,* and her translation of Bastiat's books were all published under her name. But her political and social essays and reviews were usually published anonymously, as some were signed with her initials, "LSM."

The McCord's divided their times between Lang Syne plantation in what is now Calhoun county, and their home in Columbia. Three children were born to the couple, a son Langdon Cheves McCord, and two daughters - Hannah and Louisa Rebecca. During the family's winters in the country, Mrs. McCord made a daily round of supervision on horseback as the plantation mistress. One of her daughters wrote of her: "She was one of the many Southern women who took their responsibilities very seriously and devoted time and thought to the welfare and happiness of her servants, as well as to the prosperity of her home." A foreign visitor to Lang Syne, Dr. E.D. Worthington of Canada, reported of Mrs. McCord in a letter:

"If any of the Negroes were sick, she had the medicine chest and dispensed liberally." Dr. Worthington went on to describe how she cured lameness in a servant boy named Ben with his help, noting how tenderly the child was cared for.

As a thinker, Louisa McCord was conservative and classical. She detested abolitionists, feminists, and socialists. According to the historian Robert Duncan Bass, Louisa McCord's translation of Frederic Bastiat's book in 1848 influenced all her subsequent political thinking. Bass wrote: "Her essays - polemic, satiric, and always clear and coherent - were conservative, pro-slavery, and pro-Southern. Her ideal was a South with a Southern culture, classic learning, with economic independence based on slavery and cotton." In her polemical writings, Louisa McCord dealt chiefly with three subjects: slavery, women, and political economy. The subject she wrote about most extensively was slavery, and she wrote to defend it. She regarded slavery, at least as it was practiced in the American South, as a benevolent institution beneficial to both master and slave. She believed, like most Americans of her time, that there was an inequality between the races. And like Abraham Lincoln, she assigned the superior position to the white race. In her essay entitled *Diversity of the Races,* published in the *Southern Quarterly Review* in 1851, she appealed to current scientific thought on the subject. She quoted from Dr. Samuel George Morton of Philadelphia, his protégé Louis Agassiz of Harvard, and other men of science. Louis Agassiz, one of the most famous scientists in the world at the time, theorized that the races came from separate origins, that is separate creations, and were endowed with unequal attributes. This theory was known as "polygenism" or "polygenesis." It might be less surprising to find such views being advanced by a Southern woman of the mid-nineteenth century when we consider that, according to the scientist Joseph LeConte of South Carolina, Louisa McCord's brilliant father, Langdon

Cheves had articulated the idea of natural selection before Charles Darwin's famous work on that subject was published.

In his autobiography, Joseph LeConte wrote of a conversation he had with Langdon Cheves concerning the origin of species. Cheves, he recalled, advanced the idea "that intermediate links would be killed off in a struggle for life as less suited to the environment. In other words, that only the fittest would survive. It must be remembered that this was before the publication of Darwin's book." LeConte said that the idea was totally new to him, and struck him very forcibly. To those who might wonder why Langdon Cheves did not publish this idea, Professor LeConte offered this explanation: "No one well-acquainted with the Southern people, and especially with the Southern planters, would ask such a question. Nothing could be more remarkable than the wide reading, the deep reflection, the refined culture, and the originality of thought and observation, that was characteristic of them. And yet the idea of publication never even entered their minds."

Like her father, Louisa McCord probably had some conversations with professor LeConte, who had been a student of Louis Agassiz at Harvard. While holding Christianity and the Bible sacred and true, Mrs. McCord rejected literalism and agreed with Agassiz that mankind had a plurality of origins in the distant past. In espousing such views, however, she differed with two learned men of Charleston, both clergymen who maintained the more orthodox view that humankind had a single origin. These were Dr. John Bachman, a Lutheran minister and naturalist who collaborated with John James Audubon, and Dr. Thomas Smith, an Irish-born Presbyterian minister and author. Both men published books in 1850 upholding the unity of the races.

Louisa McCord's review of *Uncle Tom's Cabin,* that appeared in the *Southern Quarterly Review* in 1853 was a lengthy, scathing critique of Harriet Beecher Stowe's novel. She went into many particulars of the book to refute Mrs. Stowe's depiction of Southern slavery, but I think her views can best be summed up, at least informally, by this extract from a letter Mrs. McCord wrote to a female cousin in Philadelphia in 1852.

"Oh, Mrs. Stowe, one word of that abominable woman's abominable book. I have read it lately and I'm quite shocked at you, my dear cousin, Miss Mary C. Dulles, for thinking it a strong exposition against slavery. It is one mass of fanatical bitterness and foul misrepresentation wrapped in the garb of Christian charity. She quotes the scriptures only to curse by them. Why, have you not been at the South long enough to know that our gentlemen don't keep mulatto wives, nor whip Negroes to death, nor commit all the various other enormities that she describes. She does not know what a gentleman or a lady is, at least according to our Southern notions, any more than I do a Laplander. Just look at her real benevolent gentlemen as she means him to be, her Mr. St. Claire, or her sensible woman, Mrs. Shelley - two more distressing fools and hypocrites I have never met with. Mrs. Stowe has certainly never been in any Southern state further than across the Kentucky line at most, and there and very doubtful society. All her Southern ladies and gentlemen talk coarse Yankee. But I must stop. Read the book over again my dear child and you will wonder that you ever took it for anything but what it is, i.e., as malicious and gross and abolitionist production, though I confess a cunning one as ever disgraced the press."

During the previous decade, in a speech given to the New England anti-slavery convention in Boston in 1843, the prominent abolitionist William Lloyd Garrison had addressed these words to the slaves of the South:

"We know that you're driven to the fields like beasts. Under the lash of cruel overseers or drivers and they're compelled to toil from the earliest dawn to late at night. That you do not have sufficient clothing and food. That you have no laws to protect you from the most terrible punishments your master's men choose to inflict on you. That many of your bodies are covered with scars and branded with red-hot irons. That you are constantly liable to receive wounds and bruises, stripes, mutilations, insults and outrages innumerable. That your groans are born to us on every Southern breeze. Your tears are falling thick and fast, your blood is flowing continually, that you are regarded as four-footed beasts and creeping things, and bought and sold with farming utensils and household furniture. We know all these things."

Mrs. McCord did not agree that Mr. Garrison knew much of anything, and like many other Southerners, she was not only outraged by his false depiction of American slavery, but by his call that the slaves should resort to insurrection and violence. Unlike Mrs. Stowe or Mr. Garrison, Louisa McCord possessed an intimate knowledge of Southern slavery and she knew the laws of South Carolina that dealt with it and wrote about them in her essay *British Philanthropy and American Slavery,* that was published in *DuBose Review* in 1853. It was a response to some anti-slavery articles that had appeared in British publications. One of these, a favorable review of *Uncle Tom's Cabin,* claimed that slave owners had uncontrolled power over their slaves, who were no more than property. Mrs. McCord responded by writing that "the sweeping assertion so constantly made that our laws are, in their general barring, cruel or neglectful of the slave is entirely unfounded. The truth is that our laws are most carefully protective of the slave."

She drew from an 1848 pamphlet, published by John Belton O'Neall, *The Negro Law of South Carolina,* presenting some of the passages that refuted such claims by abolitionists. Among these were the following, quoting O'Neall: "Also slaves, by the Act of 1740, are declared to be chattels personal, yet they are also in our law considered as persons with many rights and liabilities, civil and criminal... By the Act of 1821, the murder of a slave is declared to be a felony without the benefit of clergy...The Act of 1740 requires the owners of slaves to provide them with sufficient clothing, covering, and food... By the Act of 1740, slaves are protected from labor on the Sabbath day..." and so on.

I think it's worth noting that only a year after this article was published, in 1854, two white men, one of them from a wealthy Charleston family, were executed in Walterboro for the murder of a slave.

On the subject of women, Louisa McCord was perhaps at her most conservative and traditional. She opposed suffrage for women and argued that women were best fulfilled in the domestic sphere. Her 1852 essay, "Enfranchisement of Women," was written in response to a number of articles calling for what came to be known in the 20th century as "women's liberation." In it, Mrs. McCord wrote very sardonically of women who demanded equality with men.

"A true woman," she wrote, "fulfilling a woman's duties, a high minded intellectual woman, disdaining not her position, an earnest woman striving as all earnest minds can strive to do and to work as the almighty laws of nature teach her that her God would have her to do unto her, is perhaps the highest personification of Christian self-denial, love, and charity which the world can see. God, who has made every creature to its place, has perhaps not given to a woman the most enviable position in creation, but it is the most clearly defined position, out of it there is only failure and degradation."

Women who demanded equality with men, she thought, had abandoned good sense and decency. Later, in the same essay, Mrs. McCord wrote that "women will reach the greatest height of which she is capable, the greatest perhaps of which humanity is capable, not by becoming man, but by becoming more than ever woman. The woman must raise the man by helping, not by rivaling him. Without woman, this world of mankind were a wrangling dog kennel. Could woman be transformed into man, the same result would follow. She it is who softens, she it is who civilizes, not in the meteoric brilliancy of warrior or monarch, but in the quiet, unwearied, and unvarying path of duty. Woman is neither man's equal nor inferior, but only his difference."

The third subject that interested Mrs. McCord was political economy, and in this area she was a proponent of principles known as *laissez faire*. I've mentioned her translation of Frederic Bastiat's book and his influence on her thinking. Why was Bastiat important? A modern libertarian economist, Murray Rothbard, wrote that Bastiat was "a lucid and superb writer, whose brilliant and witty essays and fables to this day, are remarkable and devastating demolitions of protectionism in all forms of government subsidy and control. He was a truly scintillating advocate of an untrammeled free market." Bastiat also emphasized the importance of private property and argued that the rights of all in society are best served when property rights are respected.

The foreword to Mrs. McCord's book, apparently written by her husband, explained the importance of its subject matter, contending that it is needful for every citizen to understand that "it is not nature but ignorance and bad government which limit the productive powers of industry, and that in fulfilling the duty of a legislature, public and not private interests should form the exclusive object of his legislation, that he is not to frame systems and devise schemes for increasing the wealth and enjoyments of particular classes, but to apply himself to discover them sources of national wealth and universal prosperity."

I think what's referred to here is what has been called "crony capitalism." The economist and author Thomas DiLorenzo has written that such government favors and subsidies were the cornerstone of the Whig party in America, and later the Republican Party along with the nationalized banking system and high protectionist tariffs. "Protectionists," wrote DiLorenzo, "have always made the case for their special interests policies by producing a blizzard of plausible sounding but incorrect theories designed to blur the public's knowledge about their true intentions." It was the object of Bastiat's book, *Sophisms of the Protective Policy*, to refute these plausible sounding but incorrect theories, these "sophisms" advanced against free trade.

Bastiat not only criticized protectionists, but also socialism and the socialistic tendencies of his own government in France. In his essay called *Government*, he asked the question "what is government?" and went on to state, "I have not the pleasure of knowing my reader, but I would stake ten to one that for six months he has been making utopias, and if so that he is looking to government for the realization of them."

Mrs. McCord's article "Justice and Fraternity," published in the *Southern Quarterly Review* in 1849, was a critique of socialism and utopias enforced by law, and it drew heavily on an article of the same name by Bastiat. She quoted him as saying:

"Political economy asked from the law universal justice and nothing more, while socialism requires over and above this that the law should guarantee the realization of its favorite dogma of fraternity, or brotherly love. We are not convinced of the possibility of enforcing brotherly love upon the world. To decree it is to annihilate it. The law may force a man to be just, but vainly would it force him to be generous. When the principle is established that fraternity shall be imposed by law that the produce of our labor shall be divided by law, without any reference in regard to the rights of labor itself, who can say where this fantastic principle will stop? On such conditions can society exist?"

Frederic Bastiat's defense of free trade resonated with Mrs. McCord as a Southerner because American protectionism in the form of the tariff had been one of the principle sources of conflict between the South and the North for many decades. It came to a head in the Tariff of Abominations and the Nullification Crisis in the early 1830s and never really went away. In 1860, when South Carolina seceded the secession convention published a document entitled *Address of the People of South Carolina.* One of its chief complaints against the U.S. government was the tariff. After comparing the position of the South to that of the American colonists in 1776, the address stated: "The Southern states are a minority in Congress, their representation in Congress is useless to protect them against unjust taxation. For the last 40 years, the taxes laid by the Congress of the United States had been laid out with a view of subserving the interests of the North. To promote by prohibition Northern interests in the production of their minds and manufacturers, the people of the Southern states are not only taxed for the benefit of the Northern states, but after the taxes are collected, three-fourths of them are expended at the North."

The Morrill Tariff bill was working its way through the U.S. Congress in 1860. It passed the House of Representatives in May of that year and passed in the Senate early the following year. It was signed into law by President James Buchanan on March 2nd, 1861, two days before the inauguration of Abraham Lincoln and it raised the average tariff rate from about 15% to over 37%, with a greatly expanded list of items like copper. The Confederate Constitution of 1861 outlaws such protectionist tariffs and the economist Charles Adams argued in his book *When in the Course of Human Events,* that the Confederacy's transformation of the South into a free trade zone was the principal catalyst for Northern aggression. The war that began in 1861 ended most of Mrs. McCord's literary efforts. She turned all her energies instead to the support of the

Confederate army and became well known and highly revered in the state for her tireless work for the soldiers. Though devastated by the death of her adored son, who died in 1863 as a result of wounds from the Battle of Second Manassas, she continued to devote herself to feeding and clothing soldiers and nursing the wounded in the military hospital in Columbia. She was the president of the Soldiers Relief Association and the Ladies Clothing Association of that city. Mrs. McCord owned a house in Columbia, which general O.O. Howard, Sherman's second-in-command, used as his headquarters when the city was occupied by U.S. forces in February 1865. Just before Howard arrived, a crowd of federal soldiers began ransacking and pillaging the house. One of them seized Mrs. McCord by the throat, throttled her, and tore a watch from her dress. When General Howard arrived, the soldiers were still at work and Mrs. McCord wrote that the general saw these men in the very act of looting.

A little while later, Howard caught some of his own men attempting to set fire to the McCord residence. He ordered them to stop, but when he saw that Mrs. McCord was nearby and had overheard him, he approached her and laid the blame on the burning cotton flying about. On one occasion, when a ball of burning cotton was found inside a back entryway of the house, General Howard commented again that it was very remarkable how the cotton kept blowing about. Mrs. McCord answered him "Yes, general, very remarkable, through closed doors." Earlier that same day, Mrs. McCord had received an ominous note urging her and her family to leave Columbia. She wrote of it: "One of my maids brought me a paper, left she told me by a Yankee soldier. It was an ill-spelled, but kindly warning of the horrors to come, written upon a torn sheet of my dead son's notebook, which with private papers of every kind now strewed my yard. The writer, a lieutenant of the army of the invasion, said that he had relatives and friends at the South and that he felt for us, that his heart bled to think of what was threatened. 'Ladies,' he wrote, 'I pity you. Leave this town, go anywhere to be safer than here.' This was written in the morning, the fires were in the evening and night."

In her recollections of the war, Mrs. McCord's daughter Louisa, later Mrs. A. T. Smythe, described the soldiers who invaded and pillaged their yard and outbuildings and then their house:

"Without any warning our back gate was burst violently open and in rushed pell-mell - crowding, pushing, almost falling over each other - such a crowd of men as I never saw before or since. They seemed scarcely human in their fierce excitement. The excitement of greed and ripping, before we could look every door was burst open and every room gutted of its contents. They robbed even the Negroes. What they couldn't take, they spoiled. We stood petrified and fascinated at the window watching. There was a terrible system and skill about it all. The only confusion was caused by their anxiety to get ahead of each other and the speed with which they dashed from side to side was wonderful. They smashed, tore, and pocketed everything they could get at."

In her memoir, Louisa Smythe also described another conversation between her mother, Louisa McCord and General Howard:

"He tried to excuse the shelling when my mother asked him how they, as soldiers, brought themselves to shell defenseless women and children in their beds by some platitudes about the sad necessities of war, and how he thought of his own children in their little beds, etc., etc. - but how this had to be in retaliation for the other methods of warfare pursued by us and then told how some promising man had been blown up and terribly injured by a submarine torpedo near Savannah. Mama listened very quietly and expressed her sorrow at anyone suffering, but said that it was a new idea to make women and children atone for the wounds and deaths of soldiers. For this, the general had no answer."

Because of General Howard's presence, the McCord home was not burned and it still exists today as a historic property in Columbia. After the war, a committee of citizens was appointed to collect testimony concerning the burning of Columbia by federal troops. Over 60 affidavits from eyewitnesses, including Mrs. McCord, were assembled. They were presented along with the committee's report to the Mayor of Columbia in November 1868, but these records inexplicably disappeared from municipal archives during the carpetbagger administration of the city. When a search was made for the original report in affidavits in 1878, they were nowhere to be found.

Like other South Carolinians, Mrs. McCord was deeply affected by the outcome of the war, which resulted in the destruction of a civilization she had tried to defend. The heart that had already been broken by the death of a son and her country was broken again when she was finally persuaded to take the hated oath to the United States in order to sell her house in Columbia. In March 1870, during South Carolina's so-called Reconstruction, she penned a poignant letter to the sculptor Hiram Powers, inquiring about a portrait bust of her father which had been commissioned before the war. In it she wrote: "We are destroyed and I fear as a people passed from life forever. The true hearted among our survivors have to look with pride only upon our sufferings and upon the graves of our dead. We fought for our rights and our liberties, our very boys were heroes in endurance and in death. But now, ground down and writhing beneath the heel of a brutal conqueror, none can even live without giving up something of the purity of his feelings by submission to the unblushing, utterly, lawless tyranny of a brutal rule and the wreck of as noble a people as ever trod God's earth, must I fear inevitably fall away from its higher characteristics."

For several years after the war, Louisa McCord lived with various relations and in 1871, she left South Carolina and resided for a while in Canada. Around 1877, she returned to Charleston to live with her daughter Louisa and her son-in-law, Augustine T. Smythe. She died in 1879 and is buried in Magnolia cemetery. I will close with a brief excerpt from a tribute to Louisa McCord written by her friend, Miss I.D. Martin:

"Her eloquent pen was devoted to her country's service, as was every fiber of her being. Perhaps her last public writing was an appeal to the women of the state to join the effort to raise a monument to South Carolina's dead of the Confederate army. When some of the women of Columbia inaugurated this movement, they naturally turned to her as their leader. The Silent Sentinel on that monument keeping guard over the deathless memories of the past does not attest more fully to the valor and patriotism of the men in the field that it does to the heroism and fidelity of the women at home. Foremost among whom was Louisa S. McCord of South Carolina."

Culture

THE SHAPING OF SOUTHERN THEOLOGY

SAMUEL C. SMITH

THERE ARE LOTS OF PEOPLE you could talk about if you wanted to talk about the shaping of Southern theology, people like John Broaddus, Boyce and others. Great Southern theologians and exegetes of scripture who should command more of our attention. But I don't think there are any two individuals that we should start with other than James Henley Thornwell and Robert Louis Dabney simply because they really are - looking at the quality of their work, the quality of their writing, the depth of their insights - just phenomenal.

Thornwell was born in 1812 in South Carolina. Born into a Baptist home, he ended up being Presbyterian. His father died when Thornwell was eight years old. He went to South Carolina College. It is said that while he was there he studied 14 hours a day and read history on Saturday for leisure. He converted in 1832, decided to go into the ministry, and went to Andover Seminary. He didn't stay there long, and left. He said, "They were an awfully new school" and that "The habits of the people there are disagreeable" and that one of the main reasons he left was that they did not offer German, Syrian, and Arabic. He transferred to Harvard. He didn't stay very long and left because of the weather.

He went back home and studied at Columbia Theological Seminary and became a distinguished minister and scholar. Some very distinguished people recognized his genius, people like George Bancroft. Bancroft said that "Thornwell was one of the most learned of the learned." He was called the Calhoun of The Church.

He became a professor at South Carolina, the president of South Carolina College and then a professor at Columbia Seminary. He died at the age of 50.

If you want to start with Thornwell's works, The Banner of Truth trust has published the collected works of Thornwell, included in that is Benjamin Palmer's biography of Thornwell.

Robert Louis Dabney was born eight years after Thornwell in 1820 in Louisa County Virginia. He was taught by his older brother and a local Presbyterian minister in Farmville Virginia. His Father died when Dabney was thirteen years old. He went to Hampden Sydney and converted at age 17 while he was there. Off and on during his education he would have to stop, go home, and work the fields just to keep his family going financially. He worked in the tobacco fields, the grain fields, and quarried stone. He rebuilt the family mill and founded a school; all at the age of 18. He took a master's degree at UVA with a concentration in Greek, Latin, French and Italian. He later studied at Union Seminary, eventually spent most of his life teaching there. Dabney established himself as an exceptional teacher and scholar. He was invited to be a professor of theology at Princeton in 1860. Charles Hodge, the famous theologian, begged Dabney to come to Princeton, but Dabney just said he simply wanted to stay home. One of the reasons he gave was he didn't want to leave his slaves. He was afraid that if he left his slaves, if he sold them; the families would be broken up and he didn't want to be responsible for that. He felt a real responsibility for them. In 1862 he became Stonewall Jackson's chief of staff.

Thomas Cary Johnson said this about him: "He was a good practical farmer, a good pastor, a good teacher, a capital member of a military staff, a skilled mechanic and furniture maker, he bound books well, and drew maps and plans for buildings." A Hodge, Charles Hodge's son, at Princeton said Dabney was the best theology professor in America. And W.G.T. Shedd, considered one of the great theologians in America said that Dabney was the greatest living theologian.

Dabney wrote a massive systematic theology. He did most of his writings during the reconstruction period. Most people associate Dabney as a crank during Reconstruction, who was upset about the loss of the war. He was, in fact, a very productive scholar during the Reconstruction period, as well as after, writing on economics, education, and psychology among other subjects.

In Richard Weaver's article "The Older Religiousness of the South" he shows that in the antebellum South, religion had at least three compelling characteristics: One, it was revealed, or based on a settled revelation, thus not based on or subject to negation. Number two was its reality or realism. It was about reality. It was not compartmentalized but it was inclusive of its faith, emotion, and nature. Number three, it was a reserved religion; that is, Southern religion understood its role. It was religion and not politics. It was *laissez faire*, thus not given to forced compliance or centralization.

In a word, Southern religion was anti-modern, in the best sense of the term. It was antithetical to the train of so called progress. Conversely, in the North, especially in New England, religion had digressed into progression. By the nineteenth century, much of the North went headlong into ultimate negation, and was therefore antithetical to reality. As a result, because New England lacked appreciation for simple assent, which requires humility, and for creation and nature it had a vociferous appetite to dominate everything. Whereas the South was the land of faith. New England, as Weaver wrote, was the land of notions. Weaver said this about New England religion: "The right to criticize and even to reject the dogmas of Christianity came at length to overshadow the will to believe them." But I would ask how did a people not necessarily known for evangelical orthodoxy during the colonial period enter the Civil War era as "one of the few religious peoples left in the western world?" And conversely, how did puritan New England, and the greater North become, in so short a time, so unorthodox? Suffice to say the South was never as unorthodox as many believed during the colonial period. And the North, especially Puritan New England, was never as orthodox as we think they were.

One of the best ways to demonstrate this older religiousness that Weaver talks about, is by looking at representative Southern theologians who had a lasting impact on the region. If we want to know what Puritans believed, we should look at the writings of people like Cotton and Increase Mather and Jonathan Edwards. We almost automatically, for example, think of Edwards as America's theologian. In fact, that's what he's called today, but it would seem that one of the criteria for choosing a representative theologian would be that his ministry had established an enduring culture in his own region. Whatever there was of the Christian in New England, it was gone within 50 years of Edwards' death. The purpose here is not to present our subjects, Thornwell and Dabney as national or global anything. They would likely rise from their graves in protest. They were far too humble and locally oriented to think of themselves in idolized global categories.

My goal in this paper, other than to introduce you simply to the life and writings of these two remarkable Southern theologians is to test the accuracy of Weaver's assessment by using Thornwell and Dabney as the principal measurements. They were the two greatest theological minds in the South and arguably in the United States.

My thesis is simple: Thornwell and Dabney illustrate admirably the older religiousness of the South as Weaver presented it. First let's start with Weaver's first point. Revelational and not negation. Weaver said this, "Man cannot live under a subtle dispensation if the postulates of his existence must be continually revised." or you keep revising your religion.

The late A.J Conyers tells of the Baptist leader in Texas, B.H. Carroll, who, as a young agnostic confederate veteran, was seeking religious truth after the war. In the religious turmoil of his life he tried to find solace in what he called "anti-Christian philosophies." He had earlier admired these philosophies for what they destroyed but now was looking for something to build him up. He needed help, he said, for a hungry heart and a blasted life. He embraced the Bible and Christianity, and rejected those anti-Christian viewpoints because, in his words, they were mere negations.

In the theological writings of both Thornwell and Dabney we find this same subtle positive approach to theology, namely that Christianity at its core is a revealed religion not subject to the whim of notion and negation. Religion based on modern reactions is no religion at all. It is rather a process of continuous elimination until nothing of substance remains. In Dabney's systematic theology, in the section on the trinity, he stated that the reason rationalists think that they can negate the trinity is because they think they can understand the trinity.

After careful and deep evaluation of that doctrine in his systematic theology Dabney wrote this, "I pray the student to bear in mind that I am not here attempting to explain the trinity. But just the contrary, I'm endeavoring to convince him that it cannot be explained, and because it cannot be explained it cannot be rationally rebutted."

Dabney saw this tendency even in some of the most orthodox of his Presbyterian brethren. Even the northern brethren, the Old School Presbyterianism, ran too quickly, he said, into the negative of their theologies. When Charles Hodge came out with a revised edition of systematic theology, Dabney wrote a 50 page critique of this work and his main complaint with Hodge's systematic theology was that it focused too much on the negative. He said "The author displays the multifarious forms of error with more fullness than his own views of what is true." In other words, Hodge was focusing too much on what was not true. And he stated: "Theology appears chiefly for the purpose of refutation."

I said to you earlier that Thornwell left Harvard as a young student because of Unitarianism, but the initial problem he had with their theology was not the content of what they believed but in how and why they came to believe it. They were obsessed with what he called "A crude compound of negative articles." That is, New England Unitarianism was reactionary to Trinitarian truth. It had no real foundations. The older religiousness at its core is based on truth accepted by faith, not figured out by reason. Or worse developed in reaction to something else.

Though not *pure fides* Thornwell and Dabney did not believe you could allow reason to be the first principal and everything else deduced therefrom. If you did, the miraculous, the unexplainable, etc., would negate truth claims altogether, because some of those things just can't be explained. After all, by its very definition in the Bible, faith is the substance of things hoped for, the evidence of things not seen. The newer religiousness on the other hand, if we could call it newer religiousness, had little settled a priori doctrine. Man was the ultimate decision maker, and could determine truth by his own rational standards. Thus, when something contrary to so called reason made an assertion like the doctrine of the trinity, it was simply negated and rejected. So, the foundational doctrine of Unitarianism is a negative. That is a rejection of a long held faith dogma. Thornwell just simply called it "pagan." He also referred to Unitarians as atheists, and identified the struggle between Christianity and atheism as one of the biggest problems of the war.

Once while visiting Harvard in 1852 Thornwell attended a faculty commencement dinner, as he informed his wife by letter "They concluded the dinner by singing the 78th psalm. This had been an old custom handed down by the puritan fathers. It was really an imposing ceremony and I should have enjoyed it very much if I had not remembered they were all Unitarians."

Negation of truth has no foundation, from the very start it is a theological disaster, and is impotent to connect man to God. It only stands in opposition to something else. In Dabney's words from the first chapter of his systematic theology "The attempt fails because error never has true method, confusion is its characteristic."

Today modern theological writing, like most areas of academia, is considered productive if it is innovative. Thornwell and Dabney did not fall into that trap. Douglas Kelly said that Dabney's theological method displayed "contempt for all innovation and speculation."

Sometimes you will hear the phrase doing theology, for Dabney and Thornwell you did not do theology. That is innovative theology. By this I do not mean they shunned imaginative and effective presentation of thought. All good writing does that. But for them theology of all things was not for experimentation. Christian theology was about faithfully explaining revealed truth, not about the latest interpretive fad. They recognized there was an inexhaustive supply of biblical truth to expand and systematize, therefore where is there time for innovation? Simply put, their contribution was that they did not seek to make a new contribution but sought to be faithful to ancient truth.

Thornwell and Dabney were not pure dogmatists as I say, the philosophical context of both men's writings had deep roots in philosophical realism, particularly in Scottish common sense philosophy. This brings us to Weaver's second point, that the older religiousness was also characterized as realism. Or as I would say, Christian realism. A faith based balance of reason, emotion, and creation.

On the surface, Weaver seems to suggest that Southern religion paid little or no attention to reason. The Southerner, he wrote, did not want a reason belief but a satisfying dogma. Although Weaver, possibly for effect, overstated his claim, he actually indicates in the same article a balanced understanding. Really what Weaver is talking about is that Southerners generally rejected the spirit of rationalism

Thornwell adopted the inductive methods of Scottish common sense as a means to bridge reason, nature, and revelation. You might say that Thornwell was first generation common sense and he learned it from Robert Henry, professor of logic and ethics at South Carolina College. Henry had studied it at Edinburgh and brought it to the South. Thornwell read Dugald Stewart and William Hamilton while at college.

E. Brooks Holifield called Scottish common sense the reliable handmaiden of Southern theology. He said, "It was not so much a set of conclusions as it was a way of thinking" A philosophical realism. A Baconian method of induction to get one started in the process of investigation.

In his first chapter on systematic theology Thornwell deals with the being of God and immediately delves into two mystic proofs of God's existence. "We can know nothing right without knowing God." He said. "He is the foundation to which all streams of speculation converged. Truth is never reached until you ascend to him. Intelligence finds its consummation in the knowledge of his name." Note that Thornwell allows for "The streams of speculation" but, he said, "They converge at a prescribed point." A certain harmonious connection between faith and reason seems to offer the most satisfying approach for Thornwell.

Faith and reason and nature all work together under God's authority. For many of Thornwell's northern counterparts however, thinking was a constant of dialectal compartmentalization. And when compartmentalized in theology, one is forced to go with one thing or the other, but not both.

Thus starting with nature to discover the being of God does not suggest that Thornwell was not downplaying the Bible and revelation as the ultimate authority, but it does suggest that he did not fear an honest investigation of God's creation. Like Thornwell's colleague and friend, the accomplished scientist James LeConte, wrote: "Nature is a book in which I revealed the divine character in mind. Science is the interpretation of his divine work." For Thornwell the study of nature was not just about inquiry and proof, it was about magnifying God. It was about appreciation for nature especially, and that it was a vehicle of worship. In the second chapter of his systematic theology he said this: "These heavens and this earth, this wondrous frame of ours and that for wondrous spirit within are the products of his power and the contrivances of his infinite wisdom. Nothing is insignificant. Nothing is dumb."

Realism informed Dabney's approach to theology as much as Thornwell's. Dabney, like both Catholics and Protestants before him, sought to understand natural theology so as to provide context for revealed theology. Dabney's theological method essentially follows Thomas Reid in seeking to prove the existence of God, not from a pure axiomatic position, or from the matrix of cause and effect.

Dabney's first chapter in his systematic theology is titled 'Natural Theology," and subtitled "The Existence of God." In this and subsequent lectures he argues for a balance between an intuitive and dogmatic approach to understanding God's existence. Dabney's biographer Shawn Lucas said this: "There was a consensus between God and human beings for Dabney that preserved the reelection of both, and yet gave God priority."

A very important topic when you talk about Scottish common sense and these men is the topic of emotion. It was typical of Old

School Presbyterianism, even those who espoused Scottish common sense, to downplay emotion and religious expression. The main reason they rejected emotion was its association with New School revivalism. But with Southerners like Thornwell and Dabney, who were themselves Old School and didn't appreciate a lot about the New School movement, emotion was not so readily dismissed. To be sure they rejected emotional excess, but emotion could be used for God's glory.

Somebody, in thinking about Dabney, asked who were the three great theologians of the South? The person giving the answer said "Well if you want oratory, go to this person. If you want deep learning go to this person. If you want to blast rocks, go to Dabney." For Dabney it was vital that we understand the proper role of emotion. The soul was a unity and not subject to compartmentalization. Thus to treat it in its unified complexity was to be faithful to reality.

Dabney stood in stark contrast. The various forms of rationalist theology that presented man as an abstraction neutralized the influence of feelings. Emotion gave context to cognition in Dabney's thinking. In 1884 he reviewed James McCaulkin's book *Emotions* in the *Presbyterian Review* and in that review he said this. "Feeling is the temperature of thought."

For Dabney the emotions were not all positive. There's a negative of emotion. A legitimate negative side to emotion, and for the sake of reality, did not ignore or spiritualize it away, as we see in Dabney's celebrated address. In 1868 at Davidson College he spoke on the practical use of negative emotions. In keeping with "the law of man's sensibility," he said: "The natural reflex of injury upon us is resentment. The man who has ceased to feel moral indignation for wrong has ceased to feel the claims of virtue. Anyone who pretends to be above anger makes me suspect that his virtue is not supernatural but hypocritical."

Dabney was what Samuel Johnson called "A good hater." His Christian realism required him to be honest and not hide negative emotion. There is such a thing too in the Bible as righteous anger. Be angry and sin not, the Bible says. Of course, Dabney is well known for not forgiving the North for the Civil War and Reconstruction. He in fact, believed it was sinful to forgive those wrongs, mainly because of his theology. He didn't believe you gave forgiveness until someone repented. Whether we agree or not with that notion, it illustrates an important point about his theology. He sought to avoid the overreaching of positive sentiment when negative sentiment was more appropriate.

He hated because he believed it was the orderly emotion called for when excessive wrong had taken place. A.J. Conyers wrote that incarnational sentiment is "the most essential character of religion in the American South." He noted that southern religion has always been dominated by that strain of theology that had a healthy respect for nature and human senses.

Weaver did not mean that Southern religion was not politically and socially engaging, it was. But older religiousness in the South knew its role in society and by nature was in line with a decentrist and volitional approach to life as opposed to being forced, imposing and activist.

There is a relatively new discipline in theological circles called public theology. According to Clive Pearson, the Associate Director of the Public and Contextual Theology Strategic Research Center, it is "concerned with how the Christian faith addresses matters in society at large." It is concerned with the public relevance of Christian beliefs. Now to be sure this area of public theology is somewhat on the chic and liberal and progressive end of evangelicalism and modern Protestantism. Conservative Protestants and conservative Catholics have been engaged in culture since the church started on a very high intellectual plane, but now that progressives do it, it becomes a respectable discipline.

Thornwell and Dabney were public theologians par excellence. A good example of public theologies is reading Dabney's *Discussions* on different topics because he brings theology to bear on just about everything. Their theology was in every way intellectually informed, but it was not for the ivory tower, nor were their writings spiritual as opposed to secular. To them, all ground was holy ground, every bush was a burning bush. Dabney, for example, saw theology as the illuminating corrective in society. Whenever he wrote on secular themes such as economics, history, and psychology, you see this coming through. And again, refer to his discussions, especially the volume called *Discussions Secular.*

Both men also believed that the reach of religion had limits in a free society. They saw ecclesiastical centralization as a reflection of the problem as it existed in the broader political climate. Some believe, for example, that Southern Presbyterians separated from the Northern Church; in fact, it was the opposite, the Southern Church was literally forced out. In May 1861, the Gardiner Springs Resolution came down from the General Assembly of the Presbyterian Church in the United States meeting in Philadelphia, requiring loyalty to the federal government. They were careful to define what they meant by the federal government - "that central administration as the visible representative of our national existence."

They were saying that the executive branch is the federal government and you must swear allegiance to Lincoln. Note, that the Constitution was not the ultimate authority here, but the executive branch after the successful Gardiner Spring vote. The Southern ministers were not there for obvious reasons. Charles Hodge, to his credit, with 47 others, dissented, saying that this caused the assembly to veer into political territories that they had no business embarking on. Protesters against Hodge's dissent said, Should we "recognize as good Presbyterians, men whom our own government, with the approval of Christendom, may execute as traitors?" This shows the dark side if I ever saw one. These good Presbyterians are thinking execution for their Southern brethren, execution sanctioned by the Church.

In December of 1861, the Southern Presbyterians convened their own General Assembly of the Confederate States of America in Augusta, Georgia. The moderator, Benjamin Palmer, said that "they were compelled to separate themselves in order to preserve the crown rights of the Redeemer and the spiritual independence of his kingdom and the Church." It was in this meeting that Thornwell gave his famous address to all the Churches of Jesus Christ throughout the Earth.

In this address, he gave two reasons why the Churches should be separate. Other than the most obvious, that they had been kicked out, Thornwell took the high road here and offered a very ironic remedy in the spirit of Christian consensus "the unity of the Church does not require a formal bond of Union among all the congregations of believers throughout the earth."

In other words, churches can be in spiritual union without one segment trying to unduly control the other. This is because the Bible does not command such control. Likewise, separate nations can be friends, he argued, and there is no reason that their churches cannot be mutually supported. You might think of Thornwell's perspective in terms of a Jeffersonian, strict construction. Thornwell's decentralization was informed by his strict adherence to the Bible as Douglas Kelley has written. Thornwell's basic assumption in developing his arguments was the hermeneutical principle that whatever is not commanded in the Bible is forbidden, which is a Jeffersonian view applied to them. Strict constructionists are by nature decentrist, so that among other things, power-hungry interlopers cannot usurp the authority that belongs to a settled compact. What worked in the Church worked in the state, but not when either tried to cross into the other sphere of authority.

Likewise, for Dabney, the entire War Between the States hinged on the problem of centralization. In his article "The True Purpose of the War," Dabney wrote that the Republican war party was not the party of Union but "the party of federal usurpation and centralization." Colonel J.B. Baldwin's narrative of his meeting with Lincoln is contained in *Discussions,* volume IV. The issue for Dabney was just as much theological as it was political. In fact, the two went hand-in-hand. Dabney's theological and secular writings are imbued with liberty as God-given and sacred, and overt centralization as unrighteous and unconstitutional. He also said the Gardiner Spring resolution was divisive of the Church and that these Northern brethren were wrong in making secession sinful. The whole affair "cannot be a proper subject for Church censures."

Conversely, Dabney believed that to not give allegiance to the state above the federal Union was itself sinful. So bound by theology and conscience, Dabney eventually saw no alternative but to secede. It should be remembered that Thornwell and Dabney were not what you would call "fire-eaters" at all. They both sought ways to prevent secession of the states. In this respect, they were followers of Calhoun's and Randolph's larger principles of Union. However, they saw liberty as more important than Union.

Union was a civil agreement among the states, created in the Constitution. Liberty was a gift from God, protected by the Constitution. The very idea that a God-given precept like liberty depended on a manmade concept like Union was ludicrous to someone who understood the Christian principles of government. Be that as it may, once secession was declared as the Southern states' best means to preserve liberty, both Thornwell and Dabney felt a holy obligation to support.

They did this not only as good citizens of their respective states, but as active Christian theologians. They supported secession, not just for regional or heritage purposes, but because Christian theology taught them that centralized power brings out the excesses of sinful humanity. Secession, like everything else with Thornwell and Dabney, was in the end a theological decision.

In conclusion, Dabney and Thornwell impacted their culture in a lasting way. Maybe that's backwards, or at least the wrong emphasis. One of the most important questions, maybe the most important question we can ask about religion in America is - why did orthodoxy take and remain in Southern culture, unlike anywhere else in America and even the world? I've talked about things like the impact of Scottish common sense on men like Dabney and Thornwell, as real as these outside influences were on both of these men, I really don't think that this takes us far enough. Many, for example, were influenced by Scottish common sense. Ideology does not create a society and philosophy does not either. Philosophy or ideology must first go through the filter of culture.

Culture establishes for the individual what is important, what should be sought, what should be sought after, and what should be shunned. Culture bursts, incubates and matures desire. Culture and place provide the necessary context that gives meaning - or reality. Thornwell and Dabney rejected innovation and negation, and accepted revelation. They rejected abstraction and compartmentalization and adopted reality. They rejected centralization and force, and embraced a reserved posture of faith.

To understand the older religiousness of the South, there is no better starting point than with James Henley Thornwell and Robert Lewis Dabney.

Awake for the Living: Lee and the "Feeling of Loyalty"

Aaron Wolf

"Remember therefore from whence thou art fallen, and repent, and do the first works; or else I will come unto thee quickly, and will remove thy candlestick out of his place, except thou repent."
–Revelation 2:5

THE ATTACK ON CONFEDERATE Monuments is a subspecies of what Richard M. Weaver called the "attack on memory." To understand why the attack on memory is a necessary part of the project of modernity is to understand why that attack will *never relent,* even *after* the last unassuming plaque honoring the Confederate dead is gouged out of a walkway and Robert E. Lee's bones are dug up from underneath the former Lee Chapel to be ground into powder and fed to jackals. By understanding the pervasive nature of this attack we may know more deeply the importance of memory, especially the way it forms and shapes love and loyalty, as well as how we might begin to recover our memory for ourselves and our children, and thereby rebuild a society that encourages virtue according to Divine design.

First, let us look at some "facts." The most celebrated destruction of Confederate monuments dedicated to a particular person involves those memorializing Robert E. Lee, the man who once gave Southern boys, and even Southern girls, their middle names. (My youngest is Peter Ambrose Lee Wolf.) Robert E. Lee was a Christian—a low-church Episcopalian—as well as a professional soldier. He inherited and owned slaves and freed slaves. He resigned his commission in the U.S. Army and commanded what was eventually called the Army of Northern

Virginia. More facts: By his own word he hated slavery, thought it bad for the Negro race and worse for whites. And by his own word he loved the Union and despised secession.

These are, as I said, "facts." There are, of course, many more true statements we could make about Lee—about his lineage, details about his service to his country. It is *actual* and *factual* that Lee wrote what follows in a letter to his sister, explaining why he hadn't been able to visit her in the spring of 1861:

> The whole South is in a state of revolution, into which Virginia, after a long struggle, has been drawn; and though I recognize no necessity for this state of things, and would have forborne and pleaded to the end for redress of grievances, real or supposed, yet, in my own person, I had to meet the question, whether I should take part against my native State.
>
> With all my devotion to the Union, and the feeling of loyalty and duty of an American citizen, I have not been able to make up my mind to raise my hand against my relatives, my children, my home. I have, therefore, resigned my commission in the army; and save in defence of my native State, with the sincere hope that my poor services may never be needed, I hope I may never be called on to draw my sword.

Look at the words: The man whose equestrian statues so many of us are inclined to defend, and so many others are foaming at the mouth to destroy, was not an ideologue of secession. He had particular concerns and convictions about it *even after* Abraham Lincoln's election, the secession of several states, the formation of the CSA, the drafting of the Confederate Constitution, and the election of Jefferson Davis. This letter to his sister was written from Arlington just over a week after Fort Sumter, and three days after

Virginia issued her Ordinance of Secession. *Even then,* he spoke of the South's grievances as "real or supposed." *Even then* he spoke of his "devotion to the Union." *Even then,* he understood that an American citizen has a duty, and his affections were virtuously habituated toward that duty.

He had a "feeling of loyalty."

Duty, however, is not rooted in abstract ideas, no matter who claims they are self-evident. Duty is man's obligation to pursue the good according to his station in life within the Created Order. And duty to the federal government dissolves when that government threatens to raise its hand against relatives, children, and home. How could there be virtue in drawing your sword against your family and your native state? And, more to our point, why would a monument to such a man, a man about whom the above-mentioned facts are indisputable, cause such great and sudden seizures of offense?

Here is Jesse Jackson's response: "There are no Hitler statues in Germany today or neo-Nazi material [*sic*] flying around. These guys sought to secede from our union, maintain slavery and secession and segregation and sedition, and so these statues are coming down and they should come down."

Such a stupefying statement, whose sentiment is shared by writers in major newspapers, politicians, university professors, public-school teachers, denominational leaders, and a growing army of snowflakes, cannot be met with facts, even though we might be tempted to offer some once our blood returns from rolling boil to simmer. For we must remember something that we, for too long, have forgotten: Facts themselves are meaningless.

"'Facts' do not exist by themselves—surely not in our minds," writes John Lukacs (*At the End of an Age*). "There is no such thing as an entirely independent, or isolated, or unchanging fact. Any 'fact' is inseparable from our association of it with another 'fact' (and in our minds this association is necessarily an association with a *preceding* fact). Any 'fact' that is beyond or beneath our cognition, or consciousness, or perception, is meaningless to us—which is why we must be very careful not to dissociate 'facts' from the way in which they are stated."

I bring this up here for a reason. Every time another Lee monument is torn down, the newspapers, magazines, and websites take another turn at calling him a traitor, and condemning him and everyone who might admire him as a racist. On that dark day at Lee Circle in New Orleans when his monument was clumsily brought down by masked men on a crane, I engaged in an online debate with a Republican editorialist about the character of Lee. Why, he wondered, would anyone want to memorialize this monster, whose image could call to mind nothing but the scourge of slavery and the hatred of black people? How could any American defend a man who had fought against the Federal Army of the United States? (His eyes had seen the glory.) I challenged him with facts. I mentioned Lee's stated dislike of slavery. I mentioned his turning down of a commission in the CSA, before Virginia seceded. I quoted the aforementioned letter in which Lee outlined his reasons for resigning his commission and clarified his understanding of duty. I mentioned Lee's insistence to his men and to anyone who would listen, after the War, that peaceable relations be pursued. I mentioned that Lee declared his happiness at the thought that slavery had ended. None of these facts mattered. Actually, it was worse than that: The facts proved his point.

Lee's very understanding of an ordered reality and a man's corresponding duty within it was outrageous to my Republican opponent, even as it was to Ulysses Grant, as Grant stated in his memoirs. But paradoxically, Grant was more sober than this 21st

Century Republican. Grant maintained deep respect for Lee; my GOP debater thought he should've been hanged.

With each new episode of the ongoing Attack on Southern Symbols, some scribe among America's Pharisees will trot out quotations from General Lee in which Lee himself indicates his disapproval of monuments to the Confederacy—again, in the interest of peace. "Robert E. Lee opposed Confederate monuments" rang the title from PBS in the wake of last year's shameful disaster at Charlottesville. In its treatment of Lee, the article is mild compared with the standard article that has emerged over the last decade, which must always include the word *traitor*. PBS does not call him that. But PBS does *suggest* as much, rehearsing his list of sins, which, in our Manichaean world of free-floating facts, comprises everything he ever did, including, remarkably, his sin of succumbing to a stroke. "Lee died in 1870," PBS states, "contributing to his rise as a romantic symbol of the 'lost cause' for some white southerners." The voicing and tense of the verbs imply that even Lee's death was an act of rebellion, providing singularly racist Southerners—*white* Southerners, you will note, servants of the Demiurge—with the inspiration they needed suddenly to redefine a war they knew they fought solely for the brutal oppression of Negroes, transforming it after the fact into an effort to preserve states' rights and protect their homes and hearths. Lee had a stroke so that he might create the Myth of the Lost Cause.

PBS even invites speculation on Lee's motives for opposing monuments to the Confederacy. It cites Lee biographer Jonathan Horn:

"You think he'd come down in the camp that would say 'remove the monuments,'" Horn posited. "But you have to ask *why*. He might just want to *hide the history*, to move on, rather than face these issues."

Jonathan Horn was also a speechwriter for George W. Bush. The Bush administration did not lack for diversity. Condoleezza Rice has come down on the opposite side of the debate over Southern monuments. She has gone on record as opposing the destruction of Southern monuments, on the grounds that keeping them up and in place is *necessary* in order for us to *avoid* the sin of "hiding the history." In her estimation, "hiding the history" means "sanitizing" it, depriving the public of the requisite and constant reminder of slavery that is needed for us to continue "expanding our definition of 'we the people.'" Monuments to slave-owners like Lee inspire us to maintain our struggle as Americans to live up to the "American Creed," which for Secretary Rice is the "aspiration" of progress, and includes as its very "lifeblood" an invitation to the world to participate in it. So the "fact" called to mind when we see Lee atop Traveller is that there is no American people, only an idea.

Secretary Rice's view is the minority view, although it is about the only defense the American Right seems capable of mounting against the refurbishing of America's public spaces in this Age of Image and Ideology. The process is now routine. The Left demands the removal of a Southern symbol, in the name of social justice and equality. The Right demurs, attempts to be conservative, and responds, "Who's next—Jefferson? Washington?" The Left agrees that Jefferson and Washington will indeed be next, but *first things first*. The Right then remembers that Congress is reelected every two years, that conservative writers like to appear on panels on the Sunday shows, that the Klan was Democratic, and that Lincoln was a Republican; and so the Right agrees that the Southern symbol must go, in the name of social justice and equality. The demolition proceeds, the flag is lowered, and Nikki Haley is promoted to the United Nations. Both sides, out of ignorance or malevolence or both, seek to "hide the history." For ultimately, both sides seek the "end of history."

The "end of history," as Francis Fukuyama portentously termed it, was supposed to come about through the spread of liberal democracy, which, by the lights of Condoleezza Rice, George W. Bush, John McCain, and Bill Kristol, no people worth keeping alive would turn down. The nations of the world will adopt liberal democratic governments, with the United States as the lead domino, and there will be no basis for any other government to arise. Others, of the Marxist/Antifa/Bernie bent, would see history's end in a socialist workers' paradise where no one goes to work and everyone attends free community college and Harvard Law School. Their history ends in John Lennon's "Imagine." (It was odd during the 2018 Winter Olympics to witness ice dancers representing the United States gliding and twizzling to the line "Imagine there's no countries / I wonder if you can," in an arena two hours from the DMZ.) Both Right and Left have the end of history as their imagined goal, and govern accordingly, each attempting to create and impose new federal laws that will align the lives of 350 million people with the fabled "American Creed," in which the hypostatic union includes the sacred word *indivisible*. But for there to be a Left and a Right, there must be a spectrum, and that spectrum has a red shift. It has always been this way, ever since the Left and the Right emerged during the French Revolution, following an act of regicide. With our so-called Civil War, it followed fratricide.

For there to be an "end of history" in the teleological sense, there must be an end put to history *qua* history. The nationalist history of America invented by Abraham Lincoln during his campaign for the presidency and handed down to the ages in the cloying rhetoric of the Gettysburg Address was the Found Cause of the Union. Its one virtue was that it allowed some room for public Southern symbols, because the Found Cause needed its Lost Cause for the clarification of doctrine. Lee could be mistaken, yet valiant and worthy of emulation. His duty could be deemed disordered, but righteously pursued. Loyalty to family and native state and region must bow to nation and perpetual union. And so, in the old nationalist history, Lee's duty could be abstracted and assimilated. The Confederate Battle Flag could be co-opted by neo-Klansmen in 1920's Indiana, even as it is now waved by white-nationalist Nietzchean youth under the banner of the Alt-Right, goose-stepping around the Lee monument in Charlottesville. (It was revealing to see video footage of Richard Spencer reading the lyrics of "Dixie" off a cellphone to a busload of fashy-haired clones on their way to that rally. None of them knew the words. They were not in their memory.) But, "the nationalist history was fake," as Clyde Wilson wrote in *Chronicles,* in an article adapted from a speech he gave at the John Randolph Club upon receiving the Good and Faithful Servant Award.

> The nationalist history was fake. It was really the history of New England Yankees, and it ignored, slandered, or coopted the stories of other Americans. Early on, the "intellectuals" of Massachusetts set out very deliberately—and you can document this with great specificity—to make the American story their exclusive property. After the War to Prevent Southern Independence, their mission was complete. The proud fox-hunting Virginia planter George Washington was turned into a prim New England saint, and the heroes of the Alamo were coopted for Lincoln's war on the South. To explore how Bostonian "American" history became multicultural/"gender" history would take many pages. I will only say that the two things are more closely related than many are willing to admit, just as debauchery and Puritanism

> are two sides of the same coin. But at least the old nationalist history had a limited fungibility. The new history has no redeemable value whatsoever.

Indeed the two histories are closely related, and I would argue that the Right's nationalist history was predestined, so to speak, to give way to the Left's internationalist ideology, which cannot really be described as history at all. It is the systematic attack on memory itself, disguised as history. For history requires what John Lukacs calls "historical consciousness." (No one "witnesses history"—a phrase often spoke today. For example, we were supposedly "witnessing history" when the Supreme Court declared that sodomy is marriage in *Obergefell* v. *Hodges*.) History is the "remembered past," remembered according to values and virtues that are the inheritance of a particular people. The story as told gives meaning to the "facts," and the story must be told to be remembered.

"Amnesia as a goal is a social emergent of unique significance," writes Richard Weaver ("The Attack Upon Memory," *Visions of Order*). "I do not find any other period in which men have felt to an equal degree that the past either is uninteresting or is a reproach to them. When we realize the extent to which one's memory is oneself, we are made to wonder whether there is not some element of suicidal impulse in this mood, or at least an impulse of self-hatred." I would include the influence of the diabolical, for the impulse to be "as gods" begins with the serpent's lie in the Garden and a certain amnesia with regard to what God really said.

What the serpent had not yet perfected in that antediluvian time was technology, the mechanization of all of life that could make possible the mass-consolidation of people, living apart from the natural restraints that hinder evil and habituate virtue. An industrialized society affords many creaturely comforts, including the illusion of unlimited freedom and equality, which are then held forth as goods or ends to be pursued. But to pursue them apart from the bounds of the Created Order is to destroy the created order, and therefore the very possibility of meaning and true joy. (C.S. Lewis and Andrew Lyle both wrote that the "pursuit of happiness" is a fool's errand; happiness is only found in the pursuit of God, according to the means He has granted.) Thus, amnesia as a goal, the fulfillment of the "end of history," is a recipe for mass-suicide. The increase in depression, our "opioid crisis," and our "broken young man" mass shooters are symptoms of the disease of chronic self-loathing.

Andrew Lytle's book *A Wake for the Living* defies genre. It is a deep family history written for his daughters, but it is also a narrative thesis on memory itself. It is remarkably hilarious and at the same time devastatingly poignant, showing us (as his chapter "The Hind Tit" did in *I'll Take My Stand*) how much we have lost of the humane society of the South, *even after* the War and Reconstruction. "If you don't know who you are," he writes,

> or where you come from, you will find yourself at a disadvantage. The ordered slums of suburbia are made for the confusion of the spirit. Those who live in units called *homes* or *estates*—both words do violence to the language—don't know who they are. For the profound stress between the union that is flesh and the spirit, they have been forced to exchange the appetites. Each business promotion uproots the family. Children become wayfarers. Few are given any vision of the Divine. They perforce become secular men, half men, who inhabit what is left of Christendom.

Lytle continues a paragraph or so later, in a vein similar to Chesterton's "democracy of the dead":

If we dismiss the past as dead and not as a country of the living which our eyes are unable to see, as we cannot see a foreign country but know it is there, then we are likely to become servile. Living as we will be in a lesser sense of ourselves, lacking that fuller knowledge which only the living past can give, it will be so easy to submit to pressure and receive what is already ours as a boon from authority.

Only a servile people would view a man's right to refuse to raise his hand against his family and his native state as a privilege granted him by his government. The head-of-household, the paterfamilias, the Hausvater, does not receive his authority over his family, or his duty to protect them and provide for them, from the state, as a "boon from authority." They are already his, as gifts from God. The family as God made it, and the sexes as God made them, are inherently and complexly hierarchical, intrinsically unequal according to station, yet equal in human dignity before God. Each member of the household derives meaning and pursues virtue not by eliminating natural distinctions, but by doing his distinct duties. The Father is not the Son, and the Son is not the Father. Yet human equality, that false moral principle of our post-Enlightened age, opposes hierarchy of any and every kind, whether societal and subject to slow change and improvement (as slavery was), or natural and unchanging, as the family is.

Any Southern symbol on public display is a witness against abstract equality. For man is not only sinful by nature but curious, and to witness public art is to have one's imagination awakened. *What does this mean? Who is this man here depicted, and what did he fight for? My friends who honor this statue, this sculpture, this plaque, this flag—they are neither racists nor neo-Nazis. This man said he would not raise his hand against his family. Neither would I . . .*

The possibility of man's perfection in this life and apart from divine grace is the underlying premise of both Left and Right. For that is what is meant by equality, whether it is the Left speaking of the equality of outcome, or the Right speaking of the equality of opportunity. Both mean—must mean—unlimited college tuition, unlimited sexual expression, unlimited "gender identification," unlimited immigration, and unlimited war. Statistically speaking, a certain population somewhere wants something it feels it is being denied. It wants the dignity of having a college diploma. It wants better healthcare. It wants to "love" whomever it wants to love. It wants people on the other side of the world to be as they are, knowing good from evil.

The pursuit of the perfection of man as mass-man, or mass-human, free of distinction and duty, is the ultimate abolitionism: It seeks the abolition of man. William Jennings Bryan foresaw this in Dayton, Tennessee. Man, as Darwin's naked ape, behaves like one. Weaver writes that the elimination of memory reduces man to an animal, a creature led about by base instinct, living in an eternal present.

"[W]hen we come to analyze the real nature of time," writes Weaver,

> we are forced to see that the present does not really exist, or that, at the utmost concession, it has an infinitesimal existence. The man who pretends to exist in this alone would cut himself off from almost everything. There is a past, and there is a future, but the present is being translated into the past so rapidly that no one can actually say what is the present. If we say that everything should be for the present, we must quickly divorce ourselves from each past moment and at the same time not attend to those subjective feelings, born of past experience,

> which are our picture of the future. The richness of any moment or period comes through the interweaving of what has been with what may be. If every moment past is to be sloughed off like dead skin and a curtain is to be drawn upon future probabilities, which are also furnished by the mind, the possibilities of living and of enjoyment are reduced to virtually nothing.

The violent, antinomian, indignant hatred of Southern monuments is understandable and was inevitable, given the rise to dominance of "presentism." Martin Luther, returning from exile after the Diet of Worms, decried the smashing of stained glass images because it robbed the illiterate of their Bible. The images tell a story. Southern images tell stories, too, which contradict America's national ideology, an ideology that is difficult to impose because it is unnatural. It is unnatural even for fallen men to hate their wives and children, to murder their brothers. It is unnatural to seek approval from a distant ruler to live life according to the long-held traditions of your people. It is unnatural to ask a president or Congress for permission to teach your own children at home, or to carry a weapon, or to buy milk from your neighbor's cow. But this is what the American national myth demands. It demands of us that we dedicate ourselves to propositions as religious dogmas, find our identity in the extreme outer reaches of our existence, and turn our feelings of loyalty upside down.

"It is memory that directs one along the path of obligation," writes Weaver.

> License is checked, or at least made self-conscious by this monitory awareness. Therefore if we wish to be free in the unphilosophical sense of freedom, we must get rid of mind. Memories inhibit us and even spoil our pleasures. They keep in sight the

> significance of our lives, which influences and inhibits action. Under the impossible idea of unrestricted freedom, the cry is to bury the past and let the senses take care of the present.

Symbols call memories to mind. In reading Weaver, I'm reminded of Paul Overstreet's song, sung by Randy Travis, about the temptation to adultery, whose chorus says, "But on the other hand / there's a golden band / to remind me of someone who would not understand."

The call to repentance in the Old Testament is always a call to *remember,* to recall to mind not some abstract maxim or idea or rule or dogma, but the living past in which God Himself dealt graciously with the people. Every act of apostasy is a violation of a covenant the LORD made in space and time. To commit adultery, or steal, or bear false witness is to forsake what God wrote with His own hand into Creation, and then again on tablets of stone.

Somewhere in the ninth century B.C., nearly the entire nation of Israel had turned pagan, assimilating to the worship of the gods of their Canaanite neighbors. All of Israel whored after Ba'al and Ashteroth, crafting idols and gathering in sacred groves, giving themselves over to licentiousness and the predations of a foreign-born pagan Queen Jezebel and King Ahab, who "did evil in the sight of the Lord above all that were before him."

The writer of 1 Kings describes Ahab's apostasy as a failure to remember: "And it came to pass, *as if it had been a light thing* for him to walk in the sins of Jeroboam the son of Nebat, that [Ahab] took to wife Jezebel the daughter of Ethbaal king of the Zidonians, and went and served Baal, and worshipped him."

Elijah the Tishbite remembered. In his supreme act of defiance against his king and an orgy of pagan priests cutting themselves and calling out to an impotent god made in their own image, Elijah called down fire from heaven, vindicating the name of the LORD. Even that involved a plea on behalf of the people's memory.

> And Elijah took twelve stones, according to the number of the tribes of the sons of Jacob, unto whom the word of the LORD came, saying, Israel shall be thy name: And with the stones he built an altar in the name of the LORD.

When he called for the fire, he invoked not simply Jehovah, but the God of their fathers, the "LORD God of Abraham, Isaac, and of Israel.

The monuments to Robert Edward Lee, and to Stonewall Jackson, and to the Confederate dead in general are not meant to be idols. They are the art and artifacts of memory, the memory of a people who lived in what Weaver called "*the last non-materialist civilization of the Western World*" (*The Southern Tradition at Bay*). Those who erected these artifacts lived amid the rubble of that civilization, now gone with the wind. We who are their descendants do not inhabit that civilization. And I would bet that John Lukacs would go further and add that there is no such thing as a materialist civilization, and C.S. Lewis would add that our modern, technocratic, scientistic education system engages in the ironic activity of cultivating barbarism.

Because of that, I am frankly stunned that the Southern monuments have remained for as long as they have. It is a testament to the memory of unreconstructed Southern people, and to what fragments remain of our former system of government, that there remains some drag on the designs of the image-breakers. But the momentum is in their favor. Recently, a District Court Judge dismissed charges against two, and found a third not guilty, for tearing down and desecrating a Confederate monument in Durham, North Carolina. They had done this in broad daylight, recorded it on video, and posted it on the World Wide Web. Defense attorneys argued that the action was *just*, despite the clear violation of the law, because the statue was a "symbol of white supremacy and an affront to the Constitutional right to equal protection under the law" (WRAL.com). Outside the courtroom the newly acquitted vowed to press on. "Sometimes folks have to take risks to challenge unjust laws."

Robert E. Lee, as I said earlier, did indeed caution against the erection of monuments to the Confederacy, in the interests of peace. After Reconstruction, the nationalist doctrine allowed for some degree of coexistence, provided that Southerners stayed in their place, and the symbolism of the Confederacy could be displayed publicly and ignored by those who disagreed. But that day is now over. Today, nationalism itself is reinterpreted as patriotism by the Right, and tarred and feathered as racist by the Left, with Southern symbols, stripped of memory and meaning, added into the mix, along with Swastikas. The so-called Far Right only encourages this confusion. It makes an idol out of symbols. It is beholden to scientism, specifically racialist theory. Neither side seeks to rebuild a non-materialist civilization rooted in tradition, family, and the pursuit of virtue. The best construction I can put on them is that they have no vision of such a world.

And rarely would they get such a vision offered to them, even in the churches we all attend. Weaver identified *contemporaneity* as a synonym for *presentism*.

Which of our churches hasn't aided and abetted the assault on memory by instituting "contemporary" services, music, and art? Which of our preachers can resist the temptation to tell endless stories from the pulpit about modern life, or force ancient texts into the mold of metaphor, reducing living narratives of God's mighty hand of salvation to facts misapplied? *What is the "Goliath" in your life? Self-doubt? Prejudice?* What sin against liberal democracy should we repent of this week? Such presentism steals memory from our children, robbing them even of the common language of faith. Each generation has to have multiple new translations of sacred texts, modifications to sacred songs, and words on screens instead of in books, so they are easier to alter from week to week. "Don't let me fall into temptation."

"To lose your language and your god surrenders all that you are," writes Lytle in *A Wake for the Living.* And so we are in danger of losing more than monuments. Public (and many private) schools are teaching an entire generation to hate themselves and their history. And perhaps even worse, modern life is now enslaved to the pixelated image and unformed thought, via the internet and the ubiquitous smartphone. These devices steal from the young the very possibility of a moment of leisure, chirping and buzzing in every quiet second. "Leisure," said Josef Pieper, is "the basis of culture." It also is the basis of St. Paul's prayer without ceasing. And ultimately, the uninterrupted moment is the opportunity of memory, when facts are arranged and filed on the shelves of tradition, connected by narrative. Constant animal interaction with social media and ill-named "texts" is the solvent of mind itself. This is the abolition of man with a speed and on a scale Lewis could not imagine, even for Uncle Screwtape.

Our middle-class addiction to the opioids of technology can be broken. We can renounce liberal democracy, fake history, fake news, and Marxism. But Jesus warned of casting out the demon and sweeping the house clean, without replacing him with something, or Someone, who is sacred. Seven demons will return and set up shop. In his Epilogue to *The Southern Tradition at Bay,* Weaver warned that the "harrowing" replacement of the liberal social order might be fascism, which might appeal to the young because it sets itself as a "protest against materialist theories of history and society." Fascism is attractive because it values achievement, poetry, and the possibility of a dramatic life. It calls on young men to be hard on themselves, which is an appeal to basic masculine desire. This, wrote Weaver over a half-century ago, is what awaits us if we fail to learn from the Old South about the contours of a non-materialist society and the meaning of our own selves. Events here and in Europe reveal his prescience.

But I propose no grand top-down political strategy. I propose, with Weaver and Lytle and Lukacs and Russell Kirk, art, music, poetry, and sacred texts. Memory, consciousness, mind, imagination—these are the things that will bring about a return to civility, because only through them can a vision for order, rooted in Creation, occur. "Take down the fiddle from the wall," wrote Lytle in *I'll Take My Stand.* But he also told stories. And not just stories about Bedford Forrest; he told stories to and about his own family, always refining them for comedy and poignancy. Above all, we must tell our children such stories, and "remember who we are," as Mel Bradford put it.

And so, I'll close with a story. My granny was born in a place called Paul's Switch, Arkansas, near the town of Bono in the Delta, to poor sharecroppers, the Peeks. Her grandfather, Levi Melton, was a private in the 2nd Mississippi (Company F) Infantry, which arrived at the scene of First Manassas at noon on July 20, 1861. After heavy losses during its initial engagement with the Yankees the following day, the 2nd Mississippi reformed and joined General Jackson's "First Brigade" in attacking the Federal batteries. They had over a hundred casualties, including 25 killed in action. Granny's grandpa did not see action that day; he was in the hospital tent with pneumonia, which he'd contracted as it spread among the troops at Winchester, before he rode the train to Manassas. The pneumonia damaged his lungs, and he was discharged before winter. There are no statues to Levi Benton Melton; but there is memory.

Granny had a wild-eyed way about her. She deliberately mispronounced words she found foreign and funny, like the Italian dish *La-GAYNE-ya.* It was funny to her that we would eat such a thing, instead of boiled turnip greens, neck bones, and cornbread. She hated television. It interfered with her talking. There was always something to report on, which, in turn, reminded her of someone who was long dead or should be. Dad and Gramp and I would be watching a ballgame or a heavyweight fight, and she would walk in and talk over it. "Oh, I see you're watching your little show," she'd begin.

She had also learned to be suspicious of TV. She suspected the people on the other end could see you and hear you, even when the screen wasn't turned on. This occurred to her suddenly during an early episode of *Hee-Haw.* Before Junior Samples gave out the number BR549, he looked directly at her and said, "I see ye there, with rollers in ye hair, in ye nightgown." And this described her present state to a T.

"Why is that white sheet always over the TV?" I asked when I was little, on a regular basis. Each time I got the same answer. Gramp rolled his eyes. *Was Granny crazy?* I wondered.

The other day, we were watching a football game, and on came a commercial for something called Alexa, a product made and sold by Amazon.com, owned by Jeff Bezos, the richest man on planet earth. It's a device plugged into the Internet that answers your questions and does things for you. It's connected to your growing profile, stored somewhere in the aether, and it's hooked up to your bank account. "Alexa, order pizza from Pizza Hut," said the guy on TV to the electronic device. Steven Crowder famously asked Alexa "Who is the Lord Jesus Christ?" and the device replied, "Jesus Christ is a fictional character." Apparently, Alexa also suffers from amnesia.

"Do you realize," I said to my children, "that in order for that thing to work, it has to be listening to you all the time? What's it doing with all of that information?" Seized with a sudden flash of memory, I turned off the TV and, for the umpteenth time, told them the story of Granny and Junior Samples.

"You is Kind. You is Smart. You is Important"

Tom Daniel

THEY SAY THAT WRITING is good for the soul, and my soul needs something good. So, I think it's time I talked about being one of the Southern white babies raised by a black maid. Sometimes, I forget that I not only grew up during the Civil Rights struggle, I grew up in the middle of it. It wasn't something that we watched on the news every evening that took place somewhere else in the country - we watched it out the windows of the car, or out the windows of the church, or out the door of our store. Or even literally in our own front yard. It was right there.

I know from talking with soldiers that their recollections of a particular battle are quite different from historical accounts written afterward. Historical accounts have a tendency to trim the edges in order to make something a better narrative and more digestible, when in fact, the real thing is usually chaotic, fluid, completely indescribable, and very hard to articulate. Things that make perfect sense in your head no longer make any sense at all when they're spoken or written down.

That's exactly the way I would describe my experience with the Civil Rights struggle. People outside the South have so many preconceived notions based on their examination of old black-and-white footage and documentaries that they often correct me on my own personal memories. People from outside the South have been fed a steady diet of the trimmed-down, tidied-up, progressively chronological version of events (including horribly simplified and unfair stereotypes) that people FROM the South are usually too mistrustful of their motives to talk to them about those times. Those of us who live here speak of those times often with each other, and then clam up whenever an "outsider" appears, because we simply don't trust them. We've been burned too many times before by people twisting our words and memories, and we've learned (the hard way) to be cautious. And I fear that many of our very poignant stories and memories will go with us to the grave, because we just don't trust other people well enough to speak candidly in front of them.

I guess the first misconception to block our openness comes from the ridiculous view that every white person in the South back then was either a freedom-rider or a Klansman. This incredibly stupid point of view is responsible for silencing a wealth of information that would be very useful to a contemporary young generation wrestling with its own cultural identity. I think the struggle of moderate Southern whites to be fair and good is an important page of American history, and the movie *The Help* is the ONLY movie I've ever seen to address the issue openly and accurately. In the movie, when the maids get to tell all their stories, you hear a lot of accounts of predictably horrible behavior by ignorant whites. However, you also get to hear some very touching examples of whites who were good, decent, fair, and treated everyone with respect and love, as well as moderate whites who simply didn't know what to do.

I was raised by a black maid. I was born in 1960, and my sisters were 10 and 7 when I was born and my brother was 6. All of us were raised by the same black maid, named Lee Crump. Both of my parents worked, and Lee Crump was our daily in-home parent. She instilled her values into us in a way that merged with those of our real parents. She disciplined us (which included whipping our butts when we needed it), but more importantly, she had carte blanche to discipline any child in our neighborhood. If Lee Crump thought you needed a butt-whipping, then you absolutely deserved to get one. And everybody's parents accepted that. I'll never forget one time when Lee Crump was whipping me with a fly-swatter, and my brother chimed in, "Don't hit him with a fly-swatter - he's not a fly." Her response was to whip HIM with the fly-swatter.

Lee Crump taught us to treat everyone with respect, no matter what color they were, and she taught us that both evil and goodness came in all colors. She also taught us that while we should treat everyone with respect, we should never demand respect from anyone else - we should always earn it.

She used to let me touch her hands over and over again, as I was totally fascinated that the palms of her hands looked exactly like mine, but the backs of her hands were completely different. There was an incredibly valuable lesson in that experience. During those times, it was also considered offensive to refer to African Americans as "black." The proper terminology back then was "negro," and the one time I made the mistake of calling her "black," she shoved the back of her hand in my face and yelled, "Boy, my skin is BROWN. I ain't black." From that, I learned that words we use to describe people matter a great deal to those people, and we should try to follow their wishes. She also let my sisters put make-up on her, just to see what happened to makeup on brown skin. I'll never forget that one of my sisters was captivated with the sight of ruby red lipstick on a face with brown skin, and she always bugged Lee Crump to surrender to her practice makeovers. Lee Crump wore a wig. Her real hair was braided tight against her head, and she wore wigs that resembled white hair (straight hair).

Lee Crump was also responsible for all the housework (vacuuming, dusting, etc.), but notice I didn't say she was required to do it all - she only had to make sure it got done somehow, and that's where we all fit in. She made ALL of us kids work as if we were her little maids. She divided the chores amongst all of us, and she wouldn't let us go outside to play until everything was done. If friends came over (or even wandered too close for safety), they were immediately drafted into service. Thanks to Lee Crump, every kid in our neighborhood was an expert on making beds, vacuuming, dusting, shelling peas and beans, shucking corn, and sweeping. To this day, I still challenge all-comers to try and shell peas better than I can do. I also distinctly remember her busting into my bedroom on a summer morning and yelling, "Boy, get yo' lazy ass outta that bed, and move it. Make up that bed. NOW! You got sweeping to do."

Lee Crump pointed out to all of us that stupidity came in all colors. She referred to many folks - both black and white - as "monkey fools." A monkey fool was the worst thing you could be, in her eyes. It meant you didn't have any sense, and nobody wanted to be called a monkey fool by Lee Crump.

She also knew absolutely EVERYBODY in town. If you walked anywhere in town with Lee Crump, your entire experience was filled with constant horn honking and greetings. I'm pretty sure she really did know everybody, and from watching her, I learned how to greet everybody with a smile and kindness no matter how crappy you felt at that moment. "Don't nobody wanna see yo' ass," was her way of saying that nobody wanted to see the bad side of you if your mood was foul. According to the wisdom of Lee Crump, you were supposed to suck it up and pretend to be pleasant whether you felt that way or not.

Lee Crump loved Martin Luther King, Jr., and hated Malcolm X (a monkey fool, in her opinion). She loved John Kennedy and hated LBJ (another monkey fool). In the front entryway of her home, there were three portraits hanging together - Jesus, Dr. King, and JFK. She loved Cassius Clay and hated Mohammed Ali. And she loved Rev. Billy Graham. My God, that woman LOVED Billy Graham.

Whenever my parents went out and she babysat for us at night, the ONLY thing on our TV set was Billy Graham.

Lee Crump had a loving husband and a daughter, and we knew all of them very well. Her daughter was the same age as one of my sisters, and they played together frequently. She had hogs at her house, and any food scraps from our table were collected "for the hogs." Lee Crump was a very vocal singer in her church, and she practiced her gospel singing around our house all day long. She introduced us to the music of Aretha Franklin, and I was probably the first white kid in my 1st grade class to know all the words to "Chain of Fools." And when our local school system was finally integrated by a federal judge's order in 1969, Lee Crump sat me down very seriously and told me what to expect from the "negro chillun."

I also learned so many things from her that I would otherwise have never been exposed to. I share a number of beliefs and superstitions of the "negro" community to this day. If you hear a hoot owl during the day someone is going to pass. I had this happen just this past year. I know which birds are good luck, which are bad, what ants crawling up a pine tree means (storm is coming, lots of rain). My style of cooking is more "soul food" than anything else and I must admit I'm very good at it.

When all of us were finally grown up, my father set her up in her own second-hand clothing store so that Lee Crump could continue to have a job. He rented a storefront for her and paid her rent, and she spent several days a week buying and selling clothes for many years.

When she died five years ago, my family was the only white family at her service (which is not at all an unusual sight at Southern black funerals, or "home-goings"). She would have loved all the preaching and all the singing. I often talk about all the wonderful things my parents did for me growing up, but I almost never mention how much I owe my social development to Lee Crump. It's too hard to talk about. It's not too emotional - it's just too hard to explain to anybody else who didn't go through the same thing. Many people who didn't grow up in this environment don't understand why the maids didn't resent us, but unless you lived it, it is so hard to explain the love and affection that was really there. An entire generation of whites were raised, shaped, and molded by black maids, and I don't think many people realize how much of a difference those maids were in molding a softer, more generous and tolerant generation of Southern whites.

Some people think of the civil rights movement as a much needed revolution, when, in fact, it took a lot more than simply passing some laws to make it a reality. Sure, there were some old die-hards for whom the past was a shaky foundation they were afraid to let go. Change, good or bad, can be frightening. But it was the overall quiet majority of Southern whites who were willing to try and make astronomical change in their lifetime that I credit with making such a radical difference. The "Negros" of the time were beyond ready to move on, but it couldn't have happened without both sides working together to make it a reality. Having been to other parts of the country, I honestly feel the South is more integrated than any of the other regions I've visited.

Thank you, Lee Crump.

THE NEO-PURITAN WAR ON CHRISTMAS

JOHN DEVANNY

Puritanism: The haunting fear that someone, somewhere, may be happy.
- H. L. Mencken

LET ANY MAN OF CONTRARY opinion open his mouth to persuade them [the Puritans], they close up their ears, his reasons they weigh not. . . . They are impermeable to argument and have their answers well drilled.
Richard - Hooker, Of the Lawes of Ecclesiastical Politie, 1594

THREE GREAT TRAGEDIES fell upon the English speaking world in the 1600s: the failure of the Cavaliers to destroy Puritanism, the failure of the Irish to destroy Puritanism, and the failure of Metacom, also known as King Philip, and his allies to eradicate the Puritan presence in North America. The Catholic leaders of Maryland welcomed persecuted Puritan refugees from Virginia, only to have their guests overthrow the Catholic aristocracy in a coup and repeal the Act of Toleration. There was a fleeting hope in the late seventeenth century that Puritanism in North America would implode and destroy itself from within. It seems that many second generation Puritans in Massachusetts Bay Colony did not wish to become members of the elect. To become one of the elect, a person submitted themselves to an interrogation, often days long, in an effort to convince the already recognized elect that, yes, you were one of them. The invasive process pried into every hidden aspect of one's beliefs, actions, and character. It made the most stringent scrutinies of Carthusian monks seem a pleasant afternoon pig-picking with a bit of light gossip. Many of the children of the first generation wanted no part, and their parents were more than happy to see the ungrateful and unelect brats suffer the unending torments of Hell. Until, that is, the brats had children, making the first generation Puritans grandparents, who now worried that their unbaptized grandchildren would be damned.

That changed things, and soon one could become a partial elect via the Halfway Covenant. Supposedly, God had already ordained the Whole Hog Covenant, though I have my doubts about this. But Puritans, being pure and elect, decided to improve upon what they believed to be God's plan. So the children of baptized, non-members of the Puritan church could be baptized, and all was well. Except it wasn't. It seems that revising and improving upon the works and decrees of the Almighty is habit forming, and pretty soon you do not need an Almighty because you are the Almighty. And thus our Puritan became a Yankee, and though he worshiped Mammon, he never stopped being a Puritan.

Which brings us to Christmas. During England's Dark Ages, 1649-1660, the Puritans were heaven bent on outlawing fun. No theaters, no chocolate houses, no this, no that, and certainly no Christmas. True, the most sour and Jansenistical Catholic might view raucous celebrations of Christmas as inappropriate and occasions of sin, but only a Puritan would view the celebration of the birth of Our Savior as *ipso facto* sinful. In the old days, Puritans argued that the holiday encouraged the worst appetites and impulses of the "lower sort," and was an idolatrous, papist plot to boot. Today's Neo-Puritan is all in favor of appealing to appetites and impulses of every sort, but he is rather keen about evangelizing the masses in his own special brand of intolerant tolerance. Which suggests that the good Reverend Hooker of the Church of England got it right when he described the Puritans as gnostics. Hooker, a gentle sort with a strong Thomistic bent, spent innumerable hours attempting to engage the Puritans of his day in discussion and debate, all for naught. The Puritans had no need of discussion, debate, and certainly not instruction from the mind of the learned

Hooker. No, they already knew! And once they got into the habit of knowing better than God, they were more than happy to rearrange the natural and divine order of things to suit their ever shifting allegiances and tastes.

So now the playful old standard, "Baby It's Cold Outside," is deemed offensive, while a certain Ms. Cardi B. is deemed "brilliant" and "creative" for crooning (or is it moaning?) about various and sundry parts of the female anatomy, on a family "holiday" television show. One might be tempted to call this a form of hypocrisy, but hypocrisy requires one to know and preach the good, but do otherwise. I am not sure that the Neo-Puritan is even capable of knowing the good. Nevertheless, the Neo-Puritans do view themselves as great social and cultural sanitizers, having now consigned "Merry Christmas" to the dustbin of offensiveness, they have turned the Holy Family into the Holy Migrants, they have decreed the term "White Christmas" as racist, and the list goes on and on. And on what authority do they do these things? Being gnostics, I suppose they are the only ones who know.

Why do the Neo-Puritans hate Christmas? They hate Christmas for many of the same reasons that they hate the South. At its essence, Christmas is the celebration of humanity's need for a savior and God's generous response in sending his only Son to share our nature, and redeem us through his sacrifice on the Cross. Thus the term Christmas, the Mass of Christ. All in all, *pace* my Baptist friends, the great feast is a bit more than just Jesus's birthday, though the Neo-Puritans would still hate Christmas if it was just that. The feast of Christmas underscores human limitation and sinfulness, and God's generous response to this human reality. As Saint Paul wrote in the eighth chapter of Romans, "For the expectation of the creature waiteth for the revelation of the sons of God." (*Vulgate*) That is, all of God's creation awaits the redemption of Christ which is the great promise of Christmas to those who serve Him. Neo-Puritans despise such talk of sin, human limits, divine revelation, and redemption.

Southerners, in general, have always possessed a clearer understanding of this reality. The Southerner did not go about seeking to build utopias, nor did he one day worship God, the next day Mammon, and the next day transgenderism. Like Adam of old, the traditional Southerner understood boundaries, limits, the important labor of ameliorating evil, and man's helplessness in opposing evil without the grace of God. Nor did he lower himself to satanic depths by deciding that he knew better than God when it came to matters of good and evil. And he understood the very real consequences of sin. That is why Southerners viewed their country as a garden, and not some abstract planned, gated community called The City on the Hill. The garden was not always well-tended. So one goes out and pulls weeds, but one does not play the foolish game of calling weeds cotton and cotton weeds.

So the traditional Southern Christmas is much more than a "happy holiday," it is a joyous celebration that despite our sins and limitations, God so loved us he sent his only Son. This joy is present in the Masses and services of the holy feast. The super abundance of this divine joy spills over into Christmas morning hunts, family reunions, gift giving, stuffed hams and sweet potato casserole, and the singing of carols. It is neither a White Christmas nor a "winter holiday;" it is what the great South Carolina author, William Gilmore Simms described as a "Golden Christmas." A Merry Christmas of hope and joy found under blue skies, soft southern breezes, and a warm sun. And as such it stands as a powerful rebuke to all dour, gloomy, and self-righteous Puritans, past and present.

Remembering the Agrarians

Thomas Landess

I HAVE BEEN ASKED to give a more personal picture of some of these Agrarians whom I knew rather than any formal explication of *I'll Take My Stand,* and that's what I intend to do, but first I'd like to give a little background on who they are and why they are still important and maybe that will make the rest a little more relevant.

I'll Take My Stand, known as the Agrarian symposium, was first published in 1930. Since that time, it has never been out of print. You have to ask yourself why people have continued to read it. There are several good reasons why the volume should have disappeared from books in print decades ago:

One, it is a quirky book. The twelve essays, written by men of varying backgrounds and talents, are uneven in quality, ranging from the fiercely polemical to the hyper intellectual. Reading it is like reaching into a grab bag of lemon drops and black walnuts.

Two, the book has little obvious thematic unity; *ex post facto* John Crowe Ransom, a quiet little man who exercised an almost frightening intellectual authority over these others, wrote a statement of principles which was published as an introduction to the essays; however, the essays themselves don't necessarily illustrate those principles, and if they do the illustrations seem almost accidental, the way Newton allegedly invented gravity. Three years after the publication of *I'll Take My Stand,* a group calling itself the Humanists published a manifesto that listed in one-to-three order the principles they championed. You won't find such an uncompromising commitment to abstraction in the twelve

Agrarian essays. To them abstraction was the enemy they rode out to engage and kill.

Three, the society they defended has long since vanished, not only in the South but in the rest of the country as well. In 1930 the United States was still a nation of small towns. About 25% of Americans lived on farms, a disproportionate number of these in the South, today that figure has shrunk to barely 1%. ADM, Mexico and South America are feeding the country while rural America has been gobbled up by developers armed with new legal weaponry supplied by the U.S. Supreme Court, so to talk or even think about a society that now exists only in the time-dimmed memory of old folks, a world that is as dead and irrelevant as the tribes of Cochise and Crazy Horse.

Four, their solutions to the problems of that day were rejected by Americans in general and Southerners in particular. *I'll Take My Stand* and *Who Owns America?* made absolutely no impact on the economic and social development of their region any other reason both as theorists and strategists, they were failures.

Five, they didn't deconstruct anything.

How to respond to these arguments, all of which are quite true? First, *I'll Take My Stand* was indeed stitched together like a crazy quilt assembled informally by letters, telephone calls and when possible, conversations. That should surprise no one familiar with rural America circa 1930. This is the way people lived, sitting on a precipice, dangling their legs over chaos, yet obedient to the inner order of the soul. Back then you lived by the rhythm of nature rather than by the unrelenting authority of the clock. Hogs and chickens can't tell time and wouldn't care if they could. The corn comes up when it pleases, helped by sun and rain, and a lot of hoeing. Fruit trees are more vulnerable when they're blooming; one light freeze can kill every blossom in a mile square orchard and send a farmer, hat in hand, off to the bank.

In such a world, you couldn't hope to plan your seasons with the same confidence that Ford planned its fiscal year, with estimated costs of production, demographic charts and graphs of projected sales. No small farmer ever told another, "My philosophy of farming can be reduced to five essential points." He planted when the weather was right and prayed. Small businesses were run just as unscientifically. Traveling salesmen called "drummers" - this was before advertising - moved by train from small town to small town. Their wares in their grips and with suitcases, they stayed overnight at boarding houses, ate dinner at big, round oak tables, slept on sagging mattresses, and called on retailers the next day. They never got down to business first, not until they talked about the weather, told a few jokes, and asked about each member of the store owner's family *by name*. Then almost as an afterthought, they open their grips, showed their samples and took orders. The trick was to seem unconcerned with money, to follow a meandering course toward the inevitable solicitation.

A good drummer could sell milk to cows and eggs to chickens. In those days, you tended to trust people rather than advertising slogans or even products. You liked "Fred" and trusted him, so you bought a dozen each of his hat pins and corsets to sell to the local ladies. By the same token, "Fred" knew that if he promoted bad merchandise, he could encounter a cold stare and a set jaw when he returned next fall. This too was the world of the Agrarians.

Likewise, Ransom and his Vanderbilt associates knew the men they asked to contribute to the volume and trusted them to have a view of the region and its problems that was consonant with their own. Such a consensus grew out of an assumed but unspoken sense of communality no longer present in the South today. I urge you to read this book, or *Who Owns America?*, and its uneven and diverse essays. If only to understand why, for 80 years, it has never been out of print.

Five quick points to remember about the Agrarians:

One, they were not utopians, which they've been accused of. It was the apostles of the new South who were the utopians. It was they who believed in a paradise of the future, as yet unrealized, to be ushered in by building factories. A future just around the corner, just over the next hill. The Agrarians wanted to preserve the world they lived in, the one they could look out of the window and see.

Two, they did not oppose industrialization per se. Indeed, they said that some industry was necessary as a counterpoint to farming. For the New South advocates, industrialization became an ideology. This attitude is what they opposed.

Three, it's untrue that none of them ever farmed. Andrew Lytle was a farmer as a young man and went back to farming in his eighties. Tate farmed, Warren's family farmed, they had all lived in rural farming communities and understood the virtues of such places. Just because you didn't live in Nazi Germany doesn't mean you can't write about it.

Four, they were not aristocratic. They specifically rejected the idea that the South ever had a near aristocracy. Their ideal family was living on a small farm in the rural South, circa 1930.

Five, they were not focused exclusively on the South. They wanted to encourage the preservation of rural America throughout the country and said so.

When Richard Weaver came to Vanderbilt to get his MA in English, he was a committed socialist; someone had indoctrinated him in undergraduate school. In those days, it happened every so often. Today it happens everywhere. Socialism is too easy to explain, too easy to understand, and at first glance, too easy to love. You can be certain that little goody two-shoes, Snow White, and the other heroes and heroines of fairy tales were all socialists. A grown-up Weaver remembered his socialist mentors as "dry, insistent people of shallow objectives."

In the mid-30s, he came to Vanderbilt University where he met and fell under the spell of the Fugitive Agrarians. John Crowe Ransom, Donald Davidson, and Allen Tate were still on the faculty and Weaver would later transfer to LSU where he met and studied under Robert Penn Warren. They were anything but dry and insistent. In *Up From Liberalism* he wrote, "I liked them all as persons, they were humane, more generous, and considerably less dogmatic than those with whom I had been associated under the opposing banner." It took him a while to move from left to right, but his perception of those men worked inside of him like an antibiotic, engaging the virus he had picked up as an undergraduate.

Eventually, he came to understand that he was cured: "I recall very sharply how, in the autumn of 1939, as I was driving one afternoon across the monotonous prairies of Texas, it came to me as a revelation that I did not have to go on professing the clichés of liberalism."

I understand how he felt. I came to Vanderbilt in 1949 a liberal of sorts, with half-formed ideas of just about everything. I had read *TIME* magazine, *The New Yorker,* and books like *Black Boy* by Richard White. I thought that Southerners were bigots and racists despite the fact that neither my parents nor their friends ever exhibited such qualities. I had not yet learned to put ideas and people together like Weaver. I chose Vanderbilt in part because of the Fugitives. I wanted to take a Creative Writing course the day I arrived. Donald Davidson taught that course and didn't admit underclassmen, so I had to wait two years. Meanwhile I had heard many stories about him, that he wanted to put everybody back on the farm, that he was a right-wing ideologue, that he was a fire-eater in class.

Then one day a friend pointed him out to me as he trudged slowly across the campus, slight of figure, hunched over, plodding carefully along the sidewalk like an old man walking on ice. He had no-color hair, wore a mud-brown suit and carried his books in a green bag. "Are you sure that's him?" I asked my friend. "I'm afraid so."

The following year, I registered in two of his classes: The Ballad and Creative Writing. At first, I thought his ballad class was dull, his delivery was low-key and matter of fact, with none of the ranting and raving I'd been led to expect. I sat in the back row and drew caricatures of him and there were other students in the class hardly paying attention. Then something he said caught my attention, and I began to listen more carefully.

He never talked about anything except ballads, and ballad scholarship. No mention of politics or the South. In those days, professors were expected to keep their political and social opinions to themselves. Davidson subscribed to that professional ethic and followed it to the letter. However, several of us came to understand that while lecturing on English and Scottish border ballads, he was also creating a parallel world for our consideration. It was a world we recognized as the one we lived in, yet he was making us see it for the first time. Most of the students missed it entirely. I remember a girl telling me as we walked out: "Mr. Davidson just rattles on about those ballads, I almost went to sleep today." I tried to explain what he was doing, but she dismissed my explanation with a toss of her lovely hair and breezed off to her next class

Like scores of Davidson's disciples, I was enthralled, he changed my life in a matter of three months. Having grown up in a sophisticated little resort town in Florida, filled with the chamber of commerce and what the chamber of commerce called "winter visitors." I never thought of myself as a Southerner, yet halfway through the ballad class, I went to the library and checked out

Douglas Southall Freeman's *Lee's Lieutenants.* Some of his disciples went even further. A graduate student in English was dating a Nashville girl, one who was no better than she should be. His intentions were thoroughly and unambiguously dishonorable. Over dinner one evening, she told him that her parents were out of town and that she would be home alone all night. He was certain his time had come. Later that evening, as they were seated on a sofa in her parlor, and he was whispering entreaties, he looked up at a painting on the wall and saw a familiar face scowling at him.

"My God," he said, "that's John Singleton Mosby, the greatest guerilla fighter in the Confederacy." "Oh," she said, "you mean great-grandfather?" Without a moment's hesitation, he went down on one knee and proposed to her. I might add that I married a farmer's daughter and felt virtuous for having done so. Davidson never mentioned Lee, the Confederacy, or the South the entire time I was in his classroom and in other classes - never. All he talked about were ballads, lyrics, the modern novel, modern poetry, and poems and short stories his creative writing students submitted.

Across Hillsborough Avenue, the education professors at Peabody were also wondering how he did it. They knew he inspired students, turned their thinking upside down, sent zealots charging into the world armed with quivers of knowledge and arrows of rhetoric. Since the Peabody teaching was no more than the application of a set of diagrammable techniques, the teachers of teachers wanted to analyze and reduce Davidson's method to a formula that could be bottled and sold.

So they registered students in his class and sent them scuttling across the street every morning, with notebooks and pencils. Invariably, they came back with blank pages. "But what does he do?" the teachers of teachers asked. "He talks." "About what?" "About ballads."

In recalling him, I believe I understand part, though not all of how he drew students to him. In the first place, he was astonishingly learned. He had read everything, not just in literary studies but in other disciplines as well. One year looking for the modern equivalent of a hair shirt, he devoured dozens and dozens of sociology books, so that he could reduce the worst of them to their absurd essence, as he did in a book called *Why the Modern South Has a Great Literature.* He knew as much about music as did Cyrus P. Daniel, the chairman of the department of music at Vanderbilt, and he could recite the history of the world if need be. It goes without saying that he knew Greek and Latin, it was required at Vanderbilt at that time.

A man who could display that kind of erudition, with all the *spretistura* of a Renaissance courtier, was bound to command the respect of brighter students. *Spretistura* was a Renaissance concept that the ideal man was supposed to be able to do many things - joust, be a diplomat, and write sonnets that were almost as good as Shakespeare's - and you were supposed to do that without even seeming to try.

But he did something else, he left subtle clues to his discussion of ballads, poetry and literary scholarship. One day he was summarizing the work of scholarship of scholars who attempted to promote a social and political agenda by doing violence to the text of the ballads. A feeble light went on in my half formed-brain. After class I rushed up to him and said "Mr. Davidson, they're doing the same thing in the Religion Department with Bible Scholarship." He nodded, "I know, I know, maybe that's why I brought it up." "Oh," I said. Those clues weren't for everybody. They were just for those whose heart was already open to their secret message. At one time scores of us, maybe hundreds, were teaching in English departments around the region, and even in the world of outer darkness, like the University of Chicago. The marvelous thing about Davidson's clues, the thing that fed the undernourished egos of the dispossessed, was the illusion that we had discovered these truths all by ourselves.

I knew Andrew Lytle better than most. I visited him a number of times at his home in Monteagle and he visited us both in South Carolina and in Dallas. He was my son's godfather. Andrew never deserted, never surrendered. It has been said by critics of the Agrarians that they never farmed, so they had no right to praise agriculture. Andrew was a farmer, as a young man he ran the family farm and could talk for hours about the problems he encountered. One of his hens fell in love with him and followed him wherever he went, refusing to roost with the others. Finally, Andrew climbed up on the bar himself and squatted there. The hen followed his example, but never laid eggs because he couldn't show her how.

When asked why he quit farming, he said it required the same kind of energies that writing fiction required. He couldn't do both, so he chose fiction. Andrew was probably the best conversationalist alive. He was a treasury of anecdotes about his family, friends, and region. He could talk every evening for a lifetime and never repeat himself. When he taught at Sewanee and edited the *Sewanee Review,* he lived in a cabin in nearby Monteagle and would hold an informal open house on Friday and Saturday evenings. The Sewanee boys would flock there in brigades to sit around the house to drink Heavenly Hill bourbon out of antique julep cups, and mostly listen or ask questions. In earlier times, they may have come in part to see his three beautiful daughters, who would occasionally float through the living room, retrieve something from the kitchen, and float back to the bedroom.

As much as Donald Davidson, Andrew was unreconstructed. Mr. Davidson admired rural New England and wrote a famous book called *Still Rebels, Still Yankees* in which he praised the similar virtues of the rural South and small-time farming in New England. He didn't hate the contemporary North. Andrew never said a kind word about New England. He didn't hate the contemporary North, he just didn't think about it. To him it was as remote and irrelevant as Finland. He felt quite different about the Yankees who invaded the South in 1861, one of whom gratuitously shot his five-year-old grandmother - possibly on orders from Sherman. To him more than any of the others, the war was still raging on quiet summer nights between the occasional grinding down of gears as trucks made their way slowly up the steep grade to Sewanee. You could sit in Andrew's front porch and almost hear the Parrot guns and Napoleons echoing from Lookout Mountain where the Battle in the Clouds was still taking place. As he told the Sewanee boys, Nathan Bedford Forrest could have won the war, had it not been for the stupidity and arrogance of Braxton Bragg and the incredibly poor judgment of Jefferson Davis.

All this highly partisan history unfolded as he sat beneath a Confederate flag almost as big as a football field. You must understand that his fierce devotion to the Confederacy had nothing to do with slavery nor did it lead to animosity toward the contemporary North. He understood and wrote brilliantly about the political conflict that lay behind the Civil War, which some people refer to as the War Between the States. Another colleague has called it the War to Prevent Southern Independence and that's absolutely right.

But like many of us, Andrew's eyes fired up when he remembered the battles and heroes - Lee, Jackson, the gallant Pelham, and most of all because he was unbeatable, Nathan Bedford Forrest. *Bedford Forrest and His Critter Company,* Andrew's biography of that great general, is one of the best narratives ever published about the war.

Most of Andrew's anecdotes - the things he talked about evenings - were about his family and often what he told was unflattering and even scandalous. He lived in a typical Southern family of that era, where the only entertainment on long winter evenings was conversation and most of the conversation was gossip. You didn't spend too much time talking about the saints in the family, they were too bland and dull. Imagine *Gone with the Wind* as a novel devoted exclusively to the married life of Ashley and Melanie. You'd throw it across the room after the first 25 pages. All those interminable evenings families talked instead of their disgraceful, perverse, eccentric members - the drunks, liars, card cheats, adulterers, thieves, and certifiable idiots. All families had them and they made the most entertaining conversation provided the children were already in bed.

Allen Tate, in a famous essay, explained the explosion of Southern literature in the 1920s, 30s, and 40s by saying that the South had reached a moment of self-consciousness, when it was forced to look backward on what it had been and look forward to what people were urging the region to become, out of the tension between those two visions. He said the novelist and poet had created great literature, it was a brilliant theory typical of Tate's critical genius and it became canon law among devotees of the so-called Southern Renaissance. It is considered a valid theory as an explanation for the outpouring of Southern fiction and poetry. I've always thought it was a lot of high blown nonsense.

When literature turned away from New York City and began to focus on small-town America, a trend for which Sherwood Anderson was in part responsible, Southern poets and fiction writers suddenly found their voice. That's where they were born. What they knew as the Southern Renaissance came into being because of the kind of conversation carried on in Andrew's living room and in the summer on his front porch. Simply a continuation of the family or town gossip, so prevalent in the region before radio and television.

Faulkner sat on a bench on the square in Oxford, Mississippi, and listened to old men talk, and make no mistake when they get the chance, old men are just as prone to gossiping as old women. That's where Faulkner got the idea for many of his best stories, from the communal memory of wrinkled codgers who knew anecdotes about great-great grandparents who had been dead a hundred years. People who live in big cities are less likely to know about their family history, as Mr. Davidson once said in discussing the same phenomenon: "Can you imagine a Hemingway character having a grandfather?" When you grew up in a small town like Murfreesboro, Tennessee, as Andrew Lytle did, you knew not only the secrets of your own family but the secrets of everybody else's. In such a world, you couldn't be too proud. While it was natural to think your folks were better than anyone else's, you could never say so except to your own kin because everybody in town knew that your great-uncle Joe had been an embezzler as mine was, or that your aunt Effie had gotten pregnant and had visited cousins in Charleston for the better part of a year.

Knowing this, Andrew told all the family secrets himself, ugly as well as the inspiring. In so doing, he recreated the world the Agrarians had attempted to preserve, not in any abstract or idealized way, but in the concrete particulars of his own experience. In his published family history *A Wake for the Living,* he recaptures that world and entertains the readers as few writers could do. He often told these anecdotes and lectures, and usually got a standing ovation at the end. He had the timing of a stand-up comedian and the presence of a seasoned actor, probably because in his youth he had actually appeared on the Broadway stage.

His impact on women was extraordinary. Once after such an appearance at the University of Dallas, Mel Bradford and I were talking to him in his motel room when the phone rang. It was one of our English majors, a pretty blonde of 20 who had written her senior paper on some aspect of Andrew's work. She was engaged to be married, but she begged Andrew to let her come to his motel room alone. "You've got to give me something to remember," she said. From snatches of conversation, we could tell what she was proposing. He tried to explain that he had no intention of allowing such a meeting to take place and she began to cry. He finally handed the phone to Bradford and said, "Here Mel, you handle this."

At the time Andrew was 67. The last time I saw him he was 90. I had flown down to Tennessee from Washington to gather notes for a biography of him. His voice was no more than a whisper, his skin was drained of moisture like old leather, and he could barely walk. It was the first time I'd seen him when he looked his age. But the anecdotes still tumbled out - his boyhood, an early romance with a girl in Virginia, his first year at Vanderbilt. He had lost his daughter Kate to cancer, and he told me about a recent visit her husband, their children and the husband's new wife had made to Kate's grave. The new wife had stepped into a sudden and inexplicable hole and had broken her leg there on Kate's grave. "I know who's responsible for that" he said.

A few months later, Tim Carlson, his all-time favorite student and a member of the Sewanee faculty brought his wife over for their daily visit. In the middle of the conversation, Andrew smiled and closed his eyes, he never reopened them.

When I was teaching at Converse College in Spartanburg, South Carolina, several of us persuaded the administration to fund a creative writing workshop during the summer session. Students would take an eight-week course taught by poet-novelist-critic, Marion Montgomery. Then the group would move to a mountain lodge owned by the college where they would be joined by a fiction writer and a poet who would discuss student manuscripts and otherwise discourse on the supreme theme of art and song. It was a good way for faculty and students to use up a summer.

By then, I knew Andrew quite well and asked him to be our fiction writer, and since he knew Allen Tate quite well, we decided that Tate would be a good poet. Allen had been a Phi Delta Theta at Vanderbilt, my father's fraternity, and I had a picture of the Brotherhood that included both Allen and my father. In order to play on his heartstrings, I sent the picture along with an invitation to join our summer faculty. He wrote back a gracious letter telling me how touched he was to receive the photo, and agreeing to come that summer. I later found out he already had the identical photograph. We put together a brochure mailed to English departments throughout the country and waited for applications. We got some, enough to justify the program. A week before the scheduled arrival of our novelist and poet, I got a call from Andrew.

"I ought to tell you I don't that that one's coming." "Of course, he's coming" I said, "I have his letter." "I think he plans to go to Italy instead," he told me. I was shocked. Had I known Allen a little better, I wouldn't have been shocked at all. Andrew managed to get an old friend, poet-critic Brewster Ghiselin, to take his place. He was a charming man who did a fine job with the students.

However, when the next year rolled around I was determined to get Tate again. He agreed to come again. I got the call from Andrew, "He's hiding from his wife; he isn't coming but I enlisted a backup a couple of months ago." My heart sank, there were and are more poets out there than the sands of the desert, most of them mediocre at best. "Who did you get?" I asked. "John Crowe Ransom." Had I known that Ransom would come I would have never bothered with Allen at the time. Ransom's work was in every anthology of contemporary poetry, whereas Tate's was not. In form, diction, and tone, Ransom's bare, carefully chiseled lyrics were as readily identifiable as those of A.E. Housman or John Donne. They will be read a hundred years from now, assuming anyone can read at that time. Ransom was one of the first poets that journeyman poets imitated on their way to discovering their own voice. Some of the early poetry of Sylvia Plath sounds like it was written by Ransom on a bad day.

He all but stopped writing verse before the end of the 1920s and published only criticism. From then on, when someone attending a public lecture asked him why he had forsaken poetry, he said in his quiet, still, Southern voice: "It's a free country." When he arrived at Spartanburg, he charmed everyone with his quiet courtesy and apparent sweetness. He was short, plump with white wispy hair and the smoothest skin I ever saw on a man his age. He had a cheerful disposition, seemed to enjoy the students and was quite convivial over drinks. In the late afternoon he was gentle hearted, gentle natured, spoke softly, and never carried a stick - big or small - or so we concluded at the time. He was editor of the *Kenyon Review,* one of the two or three most prestigious literary quarterlies in America and we wondered how anyone so kind and considerate could have had the heart to reject a manuscript.

Our plan was to allow students to eat breakfast and lunch and dinner with these men, discuss literature and other important matters, and then in a private session, have their manuscripts critiqued - the fiction by Lytle, the poetry by Ransom. I remember one student, a boy named Speer, who was barely an apprentice in the art of poetry. He came to the campus sporting a beard - not as common a practice in the early sixties as it was a few years later. I remember that in one of his poems he compared himself to Christ, arguing that Jesus was probably crucified because he wore a beard - he asked one of the Converse girls for a date and she said she wouldn't go out with him unless he got rid of that beard.

Whereupon, he immediately went to the dormitory and came back clean shaven.

The next day, Marion Montgomery, who taught the eight weeks course, had the boy. If he didn't think Jesus might have shaved off his beard to avoid crucifixion, it was a valid literary question challenging the integrity of the poem and the poet. So when Speer took his portfolio into the room to discuss it with Mr. Ransom, we shook our heads. Speer didn't return to poolside after the two hour conference, but Mr. Ransom joined us with a benign smile on his face. "Well" he said, "Young Speer intends to devote his life to poetry." We were stunned. How could he possibly think that young Speer had talent or even rudimentary skill. More to the point, how could he encourage an inarticulate, self-centered boy to waste his life writing bad verse?

At that point, we concluded that the Jesus beard poem would have been appearing in the next issue of the Kenyon Review. At dinner time, young Speer was nowhere to be seen. One of the other students told us he was sulking in his tent. "Why?" we asked. We were told that he came back, pumped up with enthusiasm, but the more he thought about what Mr. Ransom had told him, the more depressed he became. He said he'll never write another a poem. Mr. Ransom moved his brow. "Oh dear," he said, and asked for another ear of corn.

As for his tender-hearted inability to exercise critical judgment as editor of the *Kenyon Review,* I remember that I had already tested him. Several years earlier I had written three poems I thought were publishable. I decided to give first crack at them to the *Kenyon Review.* Having missed the mail at home, I took them down to Union Station in Nashville so they would go out that night, which was Tuesday. Thursday morning, I looked in my home mailbox and found the envelope containing the poems. Obviously the postman had mistakenly sent them to the return address. Then

I noticed the postmark, Gambier, Ohio, and opening the envelope I found the poems inside with a standard rejection slip. My opinion of the U.S. Post Office rose a couple of notches. I got it back one day years later. I told Mr. Ransom how quickly and efficiently he had handled my manuscript. He shook his head and said, "Oh dear."

In 1970, the University of Dallas hosted the Southern Literary Festival. Mel Bradford and I decided to ask the Fugitive Agrarians to read their works at the festival and then stay over for a private recording session on Agrarianism. Now what we planned to do was to ask for $3,500 from some donor to fund the Fugitive part, then if we could get more, we were going to do the Agrarian part and I was appointed to raise the money. I was told "Go and see Mr. Constantine, he's the man on the board who handles the fund drive which is on right now. See if he'll let you ask some people and give you some names."

I went up to see Mr. Constantine. He said, "I can't let you talk to anybody who has ever given us money because you might be taking it away from me. I can't let you talk to anybody we've never asked because we might ask him and get more than you would, but I'll tell you what I'll do: I'll give you a list of the people we've asked every year who've never given us a penny and you can try them, okay?" I said "Sure," and he said, "I'll tell you what, right across the street is a man who could give you that amount of money and it would come out of his small change drawer. You know who Bunker Hunt is?" I said "No, sir." he said "Do you know who H.L. Hunt is? That's Bunker's father" and I said "No, sir."

I was new in Dallas. H.L. Hunt was the richest man in the world, according to Paul Getty at the time, and it was probably true. Mr. Constantine said, "Now, Bunker Hunt is right across the way and I'll call to make an appointment for you and you can go over there and you can ask him and maybe he'll give you something."

I went down the other way across the street, went up the elevator, and about the 20-something floor, walked into the place. It was a little old cramped office. It was very sparse. They let me in Bunker Hunt's office, big smile on his face, he said, "What can I do for you?" So I started explaining the project. He said, "Wait a minute, you're not talking about giving money to education are you?" and I said "Yeah that's right." He said, "Oh Lord, have you come to the wrong place. I don't believe in education...I believe that education has ruined this country. I think what we ought to have less education and not more...my daughter goes over here to SMU and that worries me because she's making straight A's and I think she must be believing some of what those lefty professors tell her over there...you wouldn't believe this, I had to make her go to the Cotton Bowl. She wanted to stay home and study."

I said, "Yeah, well young people are contrary these days, but I think you're mistaken...what we need is more education about the right values. You believe your philosophy can stand up in competition with others, don't you? Well we have professors in our economics department, it's free market and our English department is conservative. We get every student. And we've got conservatives in our history department."

"Anthony Kubek." he said. "Yeah, but you've got some of those lefty professors over there too don't you?" I said, "Yes, we do and what's going to happen if you don't have any around and you don't have that dialogue that you say your side will win. And these students go out and somebody pops them with one of those arguments and they don't know how to answer it."

He said, "Hey, so wait a minute, are you telling me that you have to keep a few of those lefty professors around just to show the students what to look out for?" I said, "Yeah, exactly." He said, "How much money you want?" I said $3500 and he said "Well, I'll give you a third of it...Ms. Jones, write this fellow a check for $1666.36," and I said, "Thank you."

I started to walk out and here came H.L. Hunt, picking up litter (they didn't have a janitor). He owned that building and everything in it, including the parking lot. He charged four dollars for a space per day in that parking lot, but twelve blocks away he had found someone who would let him park there for a dollar. He parked twelve and a half blocks away and walked all the way to work, and if you think about it that's pretty good mathematics because, say there are 250 work days in a year, he pays 250 dollars and he makes a thousand dollars on that space he would have been taking. That means it's a profit of seven hundred and fifty dollars, and add that in with a billion dollars which he had.

There's also a cafeteria in there, but he carried his lunch in a brown paper bag.

Whatever, we got the Agrarians, they came and we had a marvelous time with them. I met Robert Penn Warren, and he was one of the kindest, finest, most attractive men I've ever run into. Although he was a self-styled liberal by that time, he wasn't really when he sat down with those people. It was as if they had never left Vanderbilt in 1930.

When he got up to read his poetry, he started to read and he looked down and there was Tate and Ransom and Lytle and he said, "Oh Lord, I don't want to read these poems for those people, they're the meanest critics you've ever seen in your life. You'll look at old John Ransom over there and you think he's a nice, sweet fella and he's not, he's as mean as a snake."

After the sessions had ended we agreed that our private discussions weren't worth publishing because we couldn't afford to bring in others and also because we had wanted them all to ourselves. All the intimacy, all the glory. We had excluded people who could have driven the conversations more authoritatively in the right direction. Cleanth Brooks or Walter Sullivan for example. Later, Vanderbilt held its own Agrarian reunion and it went much better. They're all fading names now, twelve men who shared for a while the illusion that they could stop the inevitable unraveling of a great society. Like Cassandra, they predicted the future and no one listened. Lytle told me in his last years that they were better prophets than they knew. Things are worse now than they ever imagined.

The problem was no one believed that the society they knew could ever be taken from them. Now it's gone forever. Perhaps the greater tragedy is that people today don't even know it ever existed.

HISTORY

A Battle for Western Civilization and the South

Boyd Cathey

ON MONDAY NIGHT, August 20, 2018, approximately 200 to 250 raucous demonstrators gathered in a mob on the campus of the University of North Carolina-Chapel Hill and proceeded to tear down the century-old statue, "Silent Sam," a monument memorializing the over 250 university students who fought and died during the War Between the States. University police, whose primary goal is to protect university property from vandals and destruction, stood down and did nothing to protect the monument, apparently acting on orders from university administrators.

All across the nation—and *not* just in the states below the Mason-Dixon Line—there is an insistent effort to take down, remove, and, at times, destroy the monuments that represent our history and heritage. Certainly, it has been the statues honoring Robert E. Lee, P. G. T. de Beauregard, Jefferson Davis, and Confederate veterans that have been highlighted most specifically as targets by this movement and featured in the Mainstream Media. Indeed, very likely a majority of American citizens not that familiar with this advancing campaign probably believe that it is *only* those Confederate symbols which are the object of this frenzied attack, and that once those monuments are disposed of, further demands for "cultural cleansing" can be blunted and contained, or will just go away.

In many ways, this temporizing approach appears to be the view of much of the establishment "conservative movement," and as well, of many leaders of the Republican Party.

It is an approach that leads to cultural suicide.

An excellent example of this pusillanimous position came recently in an article by John Hood, chairman of the board of the conservative John Locke Foundation, in Raleigh, North Carolina. In his essay on the status of the three Confederate monuments now standing on Capitol Square in Raleigh currently being challenged by the administration of Democratic Governor Roy Cooper, Hood demonstrated obvious discomfort at having to defend symbols admittedly of his own Tar Heel heritage, declaring: "Why not erect more monuments and public art to commemorate a broader range of individuals, movements, and events? That's a noble enterprise that could unify North Carolinians across the political spectrum.... There has to be a better way."

Hood was a vigorous and very vocal Never Trumper (and continues to be), whose positions on most issues mirror standard establishment Republican boilerplate. And like them he answers accusations of racism, bigotry, and white supremacy from the Farther Left, as a dog answers the dog whistle of his owner...and like how most Neoconservatives respond in fearful fright to their Farther Left critics.

What actually bothers him are *not* the ideologically-motivated attacks on the monuments as symbols of Southern heritage and history, but, as he makes clear, the *physical* attacks on them. And to prove his *bona fides* to the Farther Left, he adds his own exculpatory *mea culpas* for his state's and region's "history of hate," and points proudly to his own record of reparations (of the financial kind) for slavery, racism, and white supremacy:

Although my love of state history is broad and deep, it does not extend to the Confederacy itself, the founding principles of which I view with contempt. Not only do I celebrate the abolition of slavery, the destruction of Jim Crow, and the expansion of freedom, but I also believe these events deserve far more official commemoration than North Carolina has yet erected.... I admire the planned North Carolina Freedom Park, for example. To be constructed in Raleigh on land between the General Assembly complex and the Executive Mansion, the park would "celebrate the enduring contributions of African Americans in North Carolina who struggled to gain freedom and enjoy full citizenship." Similarly, the Z. Smith Reynolds Foundation has just announced its Inclusive Public Arts Initiative, which will fund up to 10 new projects across the state with grants of up to $50,000 each. The intent is to "share stories of diversity, equality, inclusion and equity as they relate to the people and places of North Carolina, especially those whose stories have not been or are often untold," the Foundation stated.... Indeed, the grant maker for which I serve as president, the John William Pope Foundation, helped pay for a mural painted several years ago at North Carolina Central University's law school.

Hood, like the other epigones of the establishment "conservative movement"—the "Big Con" as my friend Dr. Jack Kerwick terms them—is unwilling to engage in the intellectual battle required because, essentially, he *agrees* with the Farther Left historically and philosophically, and he is willing to temporize: just don't damage the monuments *physically*, and, somehow we can all do a "Rodney King" and get along—"There has to be a better way."

This defeatist approach—which is that of Neoconservatives generally in the cultural war we find ourselves in—puts me in mind of a quote I first heard used by my mentor Russell Kirk; it is from Hilaire Belloc's *This and That and the Other* (1912) (p. 282):

> [T]he Barbarian is discoverable everywhere in this
> that he cannot make; that he can befog or destroy,
> but that he cannot sustain; and of every Barbarian in
> the decline or peril of every civilisation exactly that
> has been true. We sit by and watch the Barbarian,
> we tolerate him; in the long stretches of peace we

> are not afraid. We are tickled by his irreverence, his
> comic inversion of our old certitudes and our
> fixed creeds refreshes us: we laugh. But as we laugh
> we are watched by large and awful faces from
> beyond: and on these faces there is no smile.

Is this not the very essence of modern Neoconservatism's—and of John Hood's-craven compliance in what is, in fact, an ignominious retreat, an insouciant giving way to the enemies of our civilization?

The standard template employed by those self-denominated "social justice warriors" is that the monuments to the Confederate dead represent "racism," "a defense of slavery," and "white supremacy." Yet, as is apparent from reports from across the nation (and from Canada and Western Europe), Confederate monuments are only a first step. After them—indeed, now concurrently with the attacks on them—come assaults on symbols memorializing Christopher Columbus, Franciscan Fr. Junipero Serra (who founded so many of the early Spanish missions in California), Andrew Jackson, Woodrow Wilson, George Washington, the politically-incorrect names of cities, towns, streets, and even colleges—any visible marker of our Western Christian civilization. The list is enlarged almost daily.

What John Hood and his Neoconservative associates do not understand...or, refuse to understand...is that their praxis leads to the imminent peril that Belloc wrote about in 1912, and to the triumphant return of the "rough beast" determined to destroy and replace Western Christian civilization that poet William Butler Yeats foresaw at the cataclysmic end of the World War I in his poem "The Second Coming" (1919): that "rough beast" held at bay for twenty centuries "vexed to nightmare by a rocking cradle" in Bethlehem, who now "slouches" as the Demon Serpent of the Old Testament to be (re)born.

The John Hoods of this world wish to have it both ways: unwilling to antagonize the dominant and vociferous voices on the Farther Left, while giving the illusory appearance of opposition to the Barbarians.

Such allies in the civilizational war in which we find ourselves are no allies at all: like the chicken in the middle of the road, they will be ground down by the cultural Marxist "semi" that comes hurtling down the highway.

And who are those who have largely inspired and motivated this multifaceted campaign of cultural destruction? And who have injected fear and fright into the hearts of not just the leadership of the Democratic Party, but increasingly have neutered real opposition from "conservatives" such as John Hood? Who are they—the proverbial tails that wag the establishment dog?

There are two groups that have played primary and critical roles in this ongoing effort and in the destruction of the Confederate veterans' memorial in Durham back in August 2017, and, more recently, in the tearing down of the "Silent Sam" monument on the grounds of the University of North Carolina:

(1) The Democratic Socialists of America, who have been at the forefront of rowdy demonstrations, petitions, and other actions aimed at removing the "Silent Sam" monument from the Chapel Hill campus. In addition to these activities, their Website (May 7, 2018) declares full support for student Maya Little and her vandalism of the monument.

(2) The Communist Workers World Party, whose members led and actively participated in the destruction of the Confederate veterans' monument in Durham, North Carolina, and who advocate "mass struggle" and "revolutionary solutions," including: "Abolish Capitalism - Disarm the Police & ICE Agents - Fight for Socialist Revolution - Defend Black Lives Matter." The

Workers World activists have turned Durham into a center of revolutionary Communist ferment. A detailed description of their actions may be found on their Web site.

These radical groups have spearheaded the efforts and mob actions, and they hold both the state Democratic Party and many Republicans in subinfeudated bondage to their rhetoric and demands. They set a linguistic narrative and policy template which have captured not just major portions of our politics, but are fawned over by the near totality of our media and are taught as unchallenged truth by our educational system and in our colleges. To dissent is to risk an organized and violent demonstration, demands for censorship, and, at a minimum, the smearing of one's reputation by the press.

Unlike John Hood and those like him, these groups and individuals fully know what they are doing and what the results would be should they succeed. They respond only to our uncompromising, intelligent, and fierce opposition.

Back in 1951 English-Cornish poet Jack Clemo (1916-1994) foresaw the age in which we now find ourselves:

The darkness comes as you foretold.
    You hear the fretful moan,
    The alien winds that rave
    As bitterly the grey truth breaks
    On disillusioned Church and frantic world.
    You see what form the judgment takes,
    What harvest faithless generations reap:
    The folds half empty, no clean pasture for the sheep;

Soil sterile where the liberal waters swirled
    Which now have hardened into mud
    Of festering ethic, fruitless hands grown chill

With their starved, pallid blood;
 And the sky freezing still." [from Jack Clemo, "The Broad Winter"]

And the poet's answer, as must be our answer:

When I saw this I chose to dwell
 With torturing symbols of the Citadel.

We must stand for—we must dwell within—our Citadel, our inheritance and culture, our very identity and being as a people representing 2,000 years of Western Christian heritage, or we shall disappear into the abyss of history.

Postscript: On Wednesday, August 22, 2018, the North Carolina Historical Commission met to take action on a proposal by Governor Roy Cooper (D) to move the three Confederate monuments (i.e., the Henry Wyatt Monument, the Monument to North Carolina Women of the Confederacy, and the Confederate Veterans' Monument) on Capitol Square in Raleigh, North Carolina, to the Bentonville Battlefield. The Commission had appointed a subcommittee at its meeting of September 22, 2017, to research the legality and advisability of such an action. The governor made his proposal purportedly based on his interpretation of the North Carolina Monuments Protection Law of 2015. But after due examination the subcommittee reported that they could find no way around the conditions set down in the Monuments law, that they were, thus, unable to approve the governor's proposal. The final vote of the full Historical Commission was 9-2, against relocation, with two members demanding that the Commission simply ignore state law.

But what the Commissioners did do was attempt to placate the Farther Left by strongly condemning racism, white supremacy, and the principles which, they declared, motivated the Confederacy—recommending that signage be erected near the existent

Confederate monuments to put them into historical "context." And that the state executive should proceed with proposing additional monuments to celebrate the state's "diversity and minorities."

It is thus obvious that the "John Hood syndrome"—and the historical and ideological narrative that sends the political and cultural establishment into paroxysms of fear, not wishing to be labeled a "racist," "white supremacist," or "fascist"—played a primary role in their considerations. Although the law prevented them from relocating the monuments, with alacrity and haste they proposed a way around those reminders of North Carolina's heritage, and it will be fascinating to witness how this latest stage in our culture war develops.

One thing, however, is certain: if it had not been for those staunch defenders of our heritage and history—mainly North Carolina Sons of Confederate Veterans, who were unwilling to compromise or give way in 2015—the North Carolina Monuments Protection Law would never have been enacted. And without that unalterable resistance, that willingness to hold high the principles and honor of our Confederate ancestors, the results of the August 22 meeting would have been entirely different.

This war—this time—is not a time for compromise or for leaving the battlefield. The battles have just begun. Either our enemies win, or we do. The options are that simple...and that stark. Our civilization and culture are at stake.

"History is nothing but a pack of lies we play upon the dead"

William Cawthon

HENRY TIMROD, the greatest Southern poet next to Edgar Allan Poe, the "Poet Laureate of the Confederacy," died during Reconstruction in 1867 at the young age of 38. Dr. James E. Kibler, an outstanding authority on all things Carolinian and a noted author and Professor Emeritus of English at the University of Georgia, tells me that Timrod died of starvation. After the war he worked as a correspondent for a new Charleston newspaper, which did not have the money to pay him. Dr. Rayburn Moore of the University of Georgia (whom I knew, a very courteous and genteel old Southern gentleman of traditional Southern values), wrote in the article on Timrod in the Poetry Foundation biographical series that after the War Timrod and his family "lived from hand to mouth, selling family furniture and silver and reluctantly accepting money from friends, including William Gilmore Simms and Hayne."

Simms himself during a time during Reconstruction lived in a garret room in Charleston with some of his children. Simms writes of having to sell prized books to have enough money to eat. He sold his extremely valuable autograph collection to Yankees to help support himself. And Simms inherited from his wife, who died during the War, a large plantation, but a plantation of even thousands of acres without adequate labour and an economy productive of prosperity cannot provide much in the way of material support other than a bare subsistence living. These times and conditions of Southern poverty after the War bred the wide known Southern expression, "Land Poor."

When Sherman's Invading Army came through Barnwell County, the Yankee soldiers burned to the ground Woodlands, Simms beautiful plantation dwelling house, except for one wing which the slaves saved by putting out the fire. Unfortunately, the wing which contained Simms' library of 10,700 volumes, one of the largest libraries of the United States, the Yankees burned to the ground, destroying Simms' exceptionally fine library.

The library of my third Great Grandfather, Dr. Horatio Bowen, of Clinton, Georgia, was also completely destroyed by Sherman's troops. The books were housed in a separate building from the dwelling house. The Yankees set fire to the library building. Reputedly, Dr. Bowen's library was one of the largest in a wide area, perhaps in all of Middle Georgia, then the leading section of Georgia. Interestingly, fine library books are in the background of an oil portrait of Dr. Bowen which an 85 year old cousin has recently entrusted to my care.

Details of the destruction of the South wrought not only by Sherman but also by many other invading Yankee armies across the length and breadth of our Southland would fill many volumes Many acts of vandalism and pure hatred of the South and destruction will be lost to history.

Southerners have been brought up with the constant refrain that the South was historically the poorest region "of the country." This has been true only since the massive Yankee conquest and laying waste of the South in the War for Our Independence as a People.

Before the War, the South was the wealthiest region of the U. S., far and away. This is not Southern pride and puffing, this is actual fact, based on the U. S. Censuses of 1860 and of 1870, which required that every head of a household give his total wealth, divided into personal and real property. In 1860, immediately before the War, the people of the South, other than the slaves – and this includes thousands of blacks who were free people – were twice as wealthy on a per capita basis as were the people of the North. Think about that! In 1870, the first Federal Census taken after the War, the people of the North were twice as wealthy as were the Southern people. Literally, for Southerners, it was a world turned upside down, in just about every way imaginable.

In 1860, every Southern State of the eleven principal Confederate States was wealthier per capita of the free population than was the wealthiest Northern State. That takes a time to really soak in. Mississippi, today the poorest State per capita, was in 1860 the wealthiest U. S. State per capita. Truly amazing, is it not? Even including all of the slaves, the wealthiest U. S. counties were Southern counties. And the slaves, though no wealth was recorded for them, did have some wealth. Many planters allowed their slaves to grow patches of cotton, which the blacks, as slaves, sold for cash, which they kept. Often planters purchased the cotton from their own slaves. The black slaves almost everywhere had their own vegetable gardens, and many planters allowed them to sell their produce at market, retaining the proceeds. The slaves also commonly hunted for game in the woods, and, again, frequently sold it if they so chose, though mainly they supplemented their diets by the wild game they themselves hunted, often with guns and rifles.

A female tutor of South Carolina was given as a present, from a slave, mauma jewelry which the slave had purchased with her own money.

So many livestock were killed by the Invading Northern Armies that the number of livestock in the entire South did not reach the pre-War levels for twenty years, or longer, even though the Southern population had increased fairly substantially between 1870 and 1880.

South Carolina did not pay off the debt the Reconstruction government had saddled her with until the 1950s.

The South has, in truth, not recovered from the economic, physical, mental, and psychological destruction and scares of the War to this day. In order to do so, the per capita wealth of the South would have to be significantly greater than that of the U. S. as a whole. Southerners would be leaders, not followers, of major trends. Southerners would not be cowed, afraid to speak their minds on subjects of the first importance. The educational level of Southerners would be far higher. Before the War, in 1860, again, with the U. S. Census figures, the proportion of Southern youth who went to college was twice the proportion of Northern youth.

Before the North's wholesale laying waste to the South, two of the best plant nurseries of the United States were Southern nurseries, the long well known Fruitland Nursery of Augusta, Georgia [the Augusta National occupies the site] and Pomaria Nursery of rural Newberry County, South Carolina, in every way as fine a nursery as Fruitland, overall offering as wide a variety and as many plants, of the same high quality, and in some areas, offering more plants.

Dr. Kibler's work has brought to light in recent decades the importance and standing of Pomaria Nursery; previously, no one except a handful of South Carolinians, had ever heard of Pomaria Nursery, just one of thousands of examples of how the South's defeat in the epic War of American history — an epic War of world history — has so impoverished the South. Much of this is our own fault. We should have cared more about and taught our own history much more than we have done. But since the sharp Leftward turn of the U. S., the most proximate origin of which was the radical decade of the 'Sixties', our public schools have been taken over to a large extent by the Central Regime which has undertaken a thorough reconstruction of Southern education. Our history in the public schools, and in many private schools as well, which often mirror much in American culture, is taught as a story of major oppression and darkness. The American Regime is literally, through many channels, destroying what remains of a distinctive South, and is nowhere more effective than in its education of Southern youth, teaching them to hold in contempt and loathing the historic South.

The crippling of the South by the North's vicious conquest goes on and on. Before the War, as the exceedingly well respected historians Eugene Genovese and Michael O'Brien have shown, Southern intellectuals in field after field matched and in some cases overmatched their Northern counterparts. Many Southern intellectuals were recognized leaders in their fields. After the War, the South was "so poor," as Southerners are wont to say, that we could barely fund education. Many of the best minds of the South had perished in the War, killed or died of disease, and, as in Timrod's case, this destruction continued after the War. Many other of the best brains of the South left the South after the War, so hopeless and helpless did the South's situation seem. The LeConte brothers, professors at both what are now the University of Georgia and the University of South Carolina before the War, left the South during Reconstruction and became major founders of the University of California, at Berkeley, the major university of California. And so it went. It has been estimated that 100,000 Southerners emigrated from the South after the War, a significant number never to return. The brilliant Judah P. Benjamin, who had served as a U. S. Senator from Louisiana and in several important Cabinet positions in the Confederate government, escaped to England where he became one of Great Britain's leading barristers. Even a son of Robert E. Lee moved to New York City, as did Varina Davis, Jefferson Davis' widow, after her husband's death. Jefferson Davis' descendants moved to Colorado, where Bertram Hayes

Davis, the principal representative of the family today, lived until a few years ago, when he moved to Dallas, Texas.

The Southern Diaspora bled the South for generations, and still does to an extent, as the major cities of the U. S. are outside the South.

We have been brainwashed to believe, and this was true to an extent even of the early generations after the War, and certainly of twentieth century generations, that the South is inferior in almost every material and intellectual facet of life. Southerners commonly joke about how poor and "country" – meaning unsophisticated and homely, for lack of a better word, we are. Now I understand that the rural life is often a very good life. Southerners of the rural and small town South have, shall we say, a wholesome acceptance of life and are traditionally a good and moral people, and ever ready to defend their personal honour. But what the defeat wrought which has been so devastating is the widespread deterioration in the belief of Southern moral superiority and, frankly, Southern intellectual superiority. The South is fully competent and capable of not only managing her own affairs in all ways, but is a leader; that we could flourish as an Independent Southern Nation in fact, if need be.

Take the case of gardening and horticulture.

Dr. Kibler says just think of the state of gardening and horticulture in the South today if we had won the War. Columbia, South Carolina, the Capital City of the Palmetto State, before the War for Southern Independence was known for its many beautiful gardens and street plantings. Sherman burned Columbia, destroying this notable aspect of Columbia.

Many accounts, not a few by Yankee soldiers themselves with the accompanying Invading Armies, noted the beauty of Southern houses and gardens and streetscapes. These descriptions were given for not only major urban centers like Columbia but also for many county seats and towns in the rural areas of the South.

The countryside was often described by the Invading Yankees as a beautiful garden, so well kept and orderly were the farms and plantations they encountered. A Yankee soldier with Sherman's columns, viewing the scene down the Macon Road from the high hill where Captain Bonner's "beautiful residence" was located (burned by Sherman) in Clinton, Georgia, described the scene as one of great pastoral beauty. S. H. Griswold, the grandson of the famed cotton gin manufacturer, Samuel Griswold of Clinton and manufacturer of the famed Confederate Colt Revolver during the War, wrote c. 1909 that before the War the Monticello Road north of Clinton was a picture of complete orderliness and beauty, a veritable "Garden of Eden," so well kept were the plantations. These types of descriptions of the Southern landscape before the Yankee hordes descended upon the South are found fairly frequently.

The picture of the Old South that Southerners have been taught is so at odds with the reality that it brings to mind Voltaire's dictum: "Don't give me history, history is nothing but a pack of lies we play upon the dead."

MONSTERS OF VIRTUOUS PRETENSION

DAVID AIKEN

WHEN I WAS A CHILD growing up in Kirkwood Baptist Church in Atlanta, Georgia, I was fascinated by three works of Atlanta public art:

The Cyclorama [and Civil War Museum at Grant Park] next to the Atlanta Zoo, is a 358 foot wide and 42 foot tall painting of the Battle of Atlanta, July 1864, the largest painting in the world - longer than a football field and taller than a four-story building. German artists painted it in Milwaukee, Wisconsin, in 1886, but in my lifetime it was permanently located in Atlanta. I was told a diorama was added in 1936, giving it a three-dimensional foreground. I remember it being restored in 1979 - 1982. It is the single most impressive painting I have ever seen, and I have seen hundreds of great paintings.

I grew up near Stone Mountain, the largest bas-relief sculpture in the world, much larger than Mount Rushmore, and the most popular tourist spot in Georgia. It is 90 by 190 feet, recessed 42 feet into the mountain. In 1916, it was conceived by the United Daughters of the Confederacy, and officially completed in 1972. Since it is carved in granite, it will last longer than any other achievement by human beings. In other words, when all the buildings, bridges, dams and engineering feats of the human race fall into ruin and dust, the granite carvings of Robert E. Lee, Jefferson Davis, and Stonewall Jackson will endure. It is fitting, I think, that the greatest ideas and the noblest heroism should be remembered in the most enduring monuments.

I learned early in my childhood that Robert E. Lee and Stonewall Jackson fought to preserve the values of men like George Washington and Thomas Jefferson – who created a culture of the soil based on inalienable rights and true learning. Robert E. Lee and Stonewall Jackson led in the fight for the American Republic of George Washington and Thomas Jefferson: for self-government and fair taxation among free and independent states. They fought with bullets.

I understood that I would have to fight not with bullets, but with books in the classroom and in the minds of people. Lacking a sound knowledge of the South, of our history and literature, we are inadequately armed when conflict arises. I learned that knowledge of key Southern authors and books is as good as musket and shot. One of the first great insights of my life is that people are enslaved with the sword and with government and private debt, but with true knowledge people are liberated.

I grew up with *Gone with the Wind* – the 1936 Pulitzer Prize winning novel by the Atlanta native Margaret Mitchell. I always knew that *Gone with the Wind* is about the Yankee invasion of Georgia and the burning and destruction of Atlanta. *Gone with the Wind* would become the most popular American novel of the 20th century, surpassing standard academic novels like *To Kill a Mockingbird* and *The Great Gatsby*, and all the other novels which are currently required reading in almost every classroom in the country. *Gone with the Wind* inspired the 1939 David O. Selznick film, which has been viewed by more people than any of the other 300,000 Hollywood films. Today it is recognized as the biggest box office hit of all time, and the pinnacle of the Hollywood system.

I should add that it also has the most quotable line in all those movies.

By the time I graduated from Murphy High School, I had read all 1,037 pages of *Gone With the Wind*, seen the movie six times, been to the Cyclorama at least 20 times, and had climbed, visited or driven by Stone Mountain hundreds of times – back in the days before the Mountain became a Georgia state park. As a youth, I lived my life around these tributes to the Southern Confederacy, without embarrassment or shame. They were at the heart of my Atlanta. I can remember buying Confederate Battle Flags at Stone Mountain, and attending the Cyclorama with my school mates.

I also knew that *Gone With the Wind* and the extraordinary film it inspired were favorites of my mother.

I vividly remember a particular scene in the middle of *Gone With the Wind.* As a child, I would catch the #18 bus from my house in Kirkwood to the downtown Loew's Grand or Paramount theaters at Five Points. I would sit there enthralled, watching and learning. At one point in the long four-hour movie, many of the people in those theaters jumped up out of their seats and cheered.

We in the theater had watched young Scarlett as a courted and pampered sixteen year old; we had seen her as a seventeen year old widow in Atlanta during the war; we had seen her nursing wounded and dying Confederate soldiers; we had seen her escape the burning city to return home to Tara where - at the age of twenty-one - she had to become the head of her surviving family and to manage the plantation of her grieving and demented father. Then we see Scarlett do something extraordinary.

A Yankee straggler rides up to the door of the big house at Tara. He enters to pillage, rape and murder. We the audience see Scarlett take the pistol Rhett Butler had given her and shoot the invader in the face. Many of the young people of Atlanta in the 1940s and 1950s would clap, and often stand up and cheer. Even as a child in elementary school, and then as a high school student, I understood.

I had learned that invaders were people who raped, burned, tortured, plundered and murdered the good people of Atlanta - my people, who went to church on Sundays; my people who worked hard, who were courteous, well-mannered, loving and loyal; my people who paid their taxes and who tried to be virtuous and fair; my people who took care of me and tried to bring me up to be responsible and respectful; my people who were deeply Southern and devoutly Christian.

To this day, when I see Scarlett shoot that Yankee criminal, coming up the stairs to steal what little remained in that looted household and to do Scarlett and Melanie physical and emotional harm, I applaud. Why? Because I learned early how to recognize a monster when I saw one. I had learned that *Gone With the Wind* is not about slavery or racism. It is not about Southern indolence or decadence, nor is the novel just a romance or a saga of the Old South. *Gone With the Wind,* rather, is about a self-righteous and greedy minority of northern Americans who captured the government and invaded, burned, looted, raped and murdered another group of better Americans.

Liberal academic critics have whined, what does Margaret Mitchell know about the destruction of Atlanta. She was born in 1900, almost half a century after the Lincoln Administration invaded the South. What did the 1940s and 1950s youth of Atlanta know, almost a whole century after Sherman marched To the Sea in Georgia, and From the Sea in Carolina? Margaret Mitchell is not a primary source, critics shout; she is a romancer, a novelist, although she was a careful historian who went to great lengths to check her facts.

Having been a college and university professor for thirty-six years, I understand the importance of primary sources. What I needed for my students was an eyewitness account, by someone who was a careful observer, who interviewed people and preserved their personal accounts in a readable narrative. What I needed was a dedicated writer, an experienced journalist and a proven historian.

I have discovered many compelling historical documents about the horrors of invasion, written by persuasive Southern authors – most of them women, or men too old, too sick, or too disabled to fight. Some of them were written by teenagers. They all talk about the human face of war waged not on the battlefield, but in undefended houses, in undefended homes, in undefended villages and plantations, and in undefended cities of civilians.

One of these historical documents is more important than all the rest. It was written by William Gilmore Simms from Charleston, the Father of Southern Literature: the South's most prolific antebellum author. Before the war Simms was an international celebrity. His books were well received and reviewed in England. Some were translated into German. One was published in Aberdeen, Scotland. Others were reviewed and collected in the last place an American would think to look for a Simms volume today. That place was Russia where works by Simms were reviewed in the mid-1800s and can still be found on display in rare book collections in both St. Petersburg and Moscow libraries.

It was actually a rather cruel twist of fate that placed Simms in Columbia shortly before Sherman's troops reached the city. Simms did not go there as a war journalist. He had no desire to become a war correspondent. All he wanted to do was find a safe place to shelter what was left of his family. His wife of twenty-seven years had just died, and his oldest son was a Confederate soldier, fighting at the front. But his youngest son was just a toddler. Simms also had a son of nine and two daughters who were still in their teens and in need of protection which Simms felt he could not provide at his Woodlands Plantation in the Barnwell District. The state capital seemed to be the safest place for them. And so it was that Simms found himself an eyewitness to the destruction of the city where years earlier he had lived and served as a state representative.

Simms's letters have been collected into six volumes. Approximately 150 of the 1,775 collected letters of William Gilmore Simms were written during the War for Southern Independence. They occupy over 300 of the 643 pages in volume IV. This fact alone speaks to the devotion of Simms as a writer, because during the war paper was hard to come by. Stamps were difficult to obtain. Simms had to make his own ink and candles. The mail was often carried from one area to another by traveling friends or family members. Near the end Simms entrusted his letters northward into the hands of soldiers returning to their homes.

Early in the war Simms wrote letters to friends in high places in the Confederate government, advising on everything from policy to fortifications of the Charleston area. He also made a valiant attempt to maintain a correspondence with close friends in the North, but as he points out mailing anything North was difficult because mail required both Confederate and Union stamps. Union stamps were almost impossible to find in the Carolina Lowcountry.

Almost thirty years of correspondence with James Lawson of New York ceases in 1861 and is not resumed until 1865, when it continues to the end of Simms's life. In the letters written to Lawson between 1860 and 1861, Simms tells us much about the way South Carolina prepared for an invasion she was certain would come.

Simms is quite eloquent in listing the misrepresentations of the South in Northern newspapers, especially in the *New York Times*:

> We crave peace. But prepare for the war that is threatened. If we are let go in peace, we shall not discriminate against the North and our trade will still be accessible to her industry and enterprise. Mr. Lincoln has spoken. And we are to have war.

I knew that in *Gone With the Wind,* the war starts - not with the bombardment of Fort Sumter — but when Lincoln calls for 75,000 volunteers to invade the South and coerce it back into the Union. The war began on April 15, 1861, when Lincoln calls for an army of volunteers, not on April 12 at Fort Sumter when South Carolina was reclaiming control of the fort recently invaded and stolen in the Charleston Harbor.

Simms is quite clear that the South did not want a war, and certainly did not start it:

> Let us not declare it. Hostilities may exist without war. Let us simply meet the issues as they arise. The consequences [of starting a war] be upon the heads of those who would not suffer us to be at peace in the Confederacy, nor leave us in peace when we withdraw from it; whose consciences made them wretched at an alliance with us, yet when we relieve their consciences of all responsibility, are unwilling to be relieved, and resolve that the victims whom they have so long robbed and reviled shall not escape them.

In one letter Simms says that he has been writing every night for six weeks until three o'clock in the morning. In addition to advising political and government leaders, he was contributing heavily to the *Charleston Mercury*. Some of his submissions were on public affairs and domestic resources. He also published poetry in this paper.

Speaking of people in his own profession, Simms says:

> I have been astonished to find that the Literary men are generally almost wholly ignorant of politics, the Constitution, the debates at the formation of the Confederation, and briefly of all the principles and issues which were involved in the establishment of the [U.S.] Confederacy.

He is talking about Emerson, Thoreau, Whitman, and Melville - the major literary men taught to our young students today.

In his letters Simms gives us recipes for making Cherry Bounce and Poor Man's Soup. He tells us that May Weed can be substituted for spinach, and Cassia for tea. He tells us that cane can be worked into mats and baskets. When it came to collecting ideas for beating the blockade by using native plants and resources, Simms was knowledgeable and resourceful.

Simms's son Gilmore was a seventeen year old cadet at The Citadel, where cartridges, cannons, and percussion caps were being made. The Cadets drilled daily. Even women and the elderly were armed and practicing to perfect their marksmanship. In a touching letter, Simms gives his son Gilmore step-by-step guidance on how to shave, carry his equipment, and conduct himself in combat. His most often repeated advice is to trust God and pray.

In reading these letters, we observe wealth and pride turning to poverty and pain. In addition to the death of his wife, four of his children die. Gilmore is wounded several times in combat and loses a finger. Yellow fever rages through Charleston. Beloved cities are reduced to ruins. Woodlands, his once grand plantation home, is burned to the ground by Sherman's men. Some 10,700 books in the library wing he built to house them at Woodlands are destroyed or carried off, along with over fifty original paintings.

At war's end, Simms lives in a garret. His remaining children are divided, some living in Columbia with him, some living in Bamberg with the Rivers family.

One of Simms's letters is particularly important. From Woodlands on December 12, 1860, on the eve of South Carolina seceding (December 20, 1860), Simms wrote a long letter to a Northern critic. On January 17, 1861, the *Charleston Mercury* published an expanded version of the letter. In it Simms justified secession on the grounds of the broken friendship between North and South: "Many Northerners," he says, "hate the South and vilify it as worthless, wanting in moral and energy; unprosperous, grossly ignorant, brutal; uneducated, wanting literature, art, statesmanship, wisdom - every element of intellect and manners." (IV, 301)

He opens this letter by stating that the people of South Carolina are not safe in this Union:

> Our safety is . . . more important to us than any Union; and, in the event of our future union with other parties, we shall certainly look to our safety, with . . . more circumspection than our fathers did, though they strove to guard their people, with all their vigilance, against the danger equally of a majority and of Federal usurpation.

Simms interprets the American Constitution framed in 1787, adopted in 1789, by the victorious Colonies as one based on friendship. He did not believe that government should promote a proposition of any kind. Instead, government should be founded on convivial order. A true Federation is based on separate and distinct states which have a compact with each other. A political order based on friendship pursues no good, no purpose. Rather, it exists for its own sake: a bond of friendship and sympathy. Friendships have no mission, no purpose. We stay in government because we are friends, not because we have some idealized world mission to accomplish, and certainly not because one section of the country becomes wealthy at the expense of other areas.

To Simms, selfish elements in the North have broken that friendship. As he says, "They [powerful and influential Northerners] have committed the greatest political and social suicide that history has ever recorded."

Employing the image of the South as feminine, Simms compares the cutting of the bonds to a woman leaving a selfish, and abusive man: She "pleaded, even while she warned! She was [ever] reluctant to proceed to extreme measures."

For thirty years now, Simms says, the South has had to put up with political and economic exploitation. Speaking for South Carolina, he continues:

> She will secede as surely as the sun shines in heaven. She will rely upon the justice of her cause and the virtue of her people. She will invade nobody. She will aggress upon no rights of others. She has never done so. The South has never been the aggressor! But we will no longer suffer aggression under the mask of "this blessed Union." We shall tear off the mask, and show the hideous faithlessness, cupidity, lying and selfishness that lurk beneath. And we shall do this, regardless of all consequences. For these we shall prepare ourselves as well as we can. . . . And on our own ground, in defense of our firesides, and in the assertion of ancestral rights, we shall deliver no blow in vain.

To Simms, the struggle against Northern aggression would ultimately be an issue of freedom: political freedom and economic freedom, self-government and free trade.

Simms was convinced that the South would thrive if freed from the jealousy, hatred and abuse of Northern aggressors:

> We, in the South, have all the essential elements for establishing the greatest and most prosperous, and longest lived of all the republics of the earth! We shall declare our ports free to the industrial energies and productions of all the world, we subject

> Northern manufactures, for the first time, to that wholesome competition with the industry of other countries, the absence of which has made her bloated in prosperity.

The Father of Southern Literature was in Columbia on February 17, 18, 19, and 20, 1865, when Sherman marched into the capital of South Carolina where some 20,000 inhabitants were living and seeking refuge. He was there when Sherman's men began to rape and to torture and to murder innocent civilians, and to plunder and to burn one of the most beautiful cities in North America. During the conflagration, Simms walked the streets, observing and remembering. Afterwards, he would interview more than sixty people, when all the horrors were still fresh in their minds.

One month later, in March 1865, Simms led the effort to publish a newspaper which included his 90-page historical narrative entitled *The Capture, Sack and Destruction of the City of Columbia* - a primary historical document on the burning and destruction of a prosperous American city. Simms listed names of Carolina people and the addresses of their destroyed property. His account is a memorial to civilian casualties. It is also the story of corruption inside American government, and a report of American violence and crime against other Americans. This important primary source almost disappeared. In 2005 (140 years after 1865) I brought it out in a book I entitled *A City Laid Waste*.

Some of this will be shocking, because I am going to let Simms speak for himself and for the people of Columbia, and the people of the Confederate South. I know of six newspaper accounts of the destruction of Columbia, but by far the most detailed, the most extensive, the most inclusive and the most important is Simms's. His account of American atrocities cannot be refuted, so lovers of Lincoln and lovers of Sherman have tried not only to discredit and repress it, but also to destroy it. The invaders became obsessed with turning their view of the war into historical record. In their determination, they ignored and then destroyed testimony which contradicted their claims.

As a result, the Jeffersonian view of America, the original vision of America dominant among the people of the founding generation up to 1861, as an experiment in justice and prosperity, has been removed from public record. International imperialism, instead, Lincoln's view of America, dominates today. Lincoln's America is currently the regnant view of American history and culture, and all Americans are consequently the poorer for the loss.

As a Revolutionary War historian, Simms sees America in terms of George Washington, Thomas Jefferson and the founding generation. He opens his historical narrative with an allusion to the Declaration of Independence and an implied question: are the human rights which our forefathers won from the British Crown being preserved or destroyed? Simms's answer is that Lincoln and his Administration are undermining the great American principle stated in the Declaration of Independence: that governments derive "their just powers from the consent of the governed." This war, this invasion, unlawful and unconstitutional - Simms says — is a death blow to American inalienable rights. How can anyone say that Americans have the right to govern themselves when you destroy our places of government? How can anyone say that Americans have freedom of religion when you destroy our churches? How can anyone say that Americans have freedom of expression when you destroy our presses and burn our newspapers? How can anyone say that Americans have the right to pursue happiness when you destroy our homes and personal property? The "cruel and malignant enemy," led by Sherman, is the antithesis of the America that the Founding Fathers envisioned and fought to establish.

We should remember that the youthful Simms studied law and passed the bar to become a practicing attorney. Throughout his life,

Simms revered the rule of law. One of the people who reviewed *A City Laid Waste* said that every cadet at West Point should not only read but also study Simms's account of the burning of Columbia.

Simms's document *The Capture, Sack and Destruction of the City of Columbia* can be summarized in a word- INVASION. Simms states the subject matter in his title, but the meaning of this important narrative is expressed in four words - Simms's four words: the invasion of South Carolina and particularly the destruction of Columbia was committed by "monsters of virtuous pretension." Monsters of Virtuous Pretension. The invasion of the South, culminating in the conflagration of Columbia, was committed by criminals who loudly proclaimed simultaneously both their innocence and their alleged pure and lofty intentions.

We should never forget that Sherman began immediately denying that he had burned Columbia. He willfully and arrogantly blamed the destruction on Wade Hampton. Simms records what he observed as well as what he received in sworn testimonies:

> Newly made graves were opened, the coffins taken out, broken open, in search of buried treasure, and the corpses left exposed. Every spot in grave yard or garden, which seemed to have been recently disturbed, was sounded with sword, or bayonet, or ramrod, in their desperate search after spoil. These ***monsters of virtuous pretension*** [bold italics mine], with their banner of streaks and spangles overhead, and sworn to the Constitution, which they neither understand nor read, never once forget the greed of appetite which has distinguished Puritanic New England for three hundred years; and, lest they might forget, the appetite is kept lively by their women - letters found upon their dead, or upon prisoners, almost invariable appealing to them to

> bring home the gauds and jewelry, even the dresses of the Southern women, to deck the fond feminine expectants at home, whom we may suppose to be all the while at their devotions, assailing Heaven with prayer in behalf of their thrice blessed cause and country.

Subsequently, the whole of American history and American literature has been dedicated to defending monsters, to sanitizing, to whitewashing, to glorifying criminals. In my lifetime, American higher educated has been slavishly committed to the outrageous premise that the invasion of the South was a good thing, and the people who perpetrated that invasion were virtuous people. Lincoln and his Administration along with Sherman, and all the officers, sergeants and privates who were active in that enormity are heroes, so we teach American students today. And anybody who disagrees with this imperial bias, anybody who questions the fundamental premise, is called names - racist, ignorant, unqualified, out of date, imbalanced, unprogressive, un-American and domestic terrorist.

Any historical document that disagrees is ignored, or destroyed. That's why Simms's account of invading "monsters of virtuous pretension" was neglected for 140 years, and almost destroyed, resulting not in a fair and historical report, but in unexamined and unconfirmed assertions of Northern righteousness and Southern degeneracy, as if Americans are not supposed to know any history, as if knowing the past makes Americans incapable of seeing grand universal principles.

More importantly, though, eyewitness sources contradict American romantic myths about Lincoln and Mr. Lincoln's War. Listen to Simms's detailed account of some of the sufferings of the people of Carolina:

The march of the enemy into our State was characterized by such scenes of brutality, license, plunder and general conflagration, as very soon showed that the threat of the Northern press, and of their soldiery, were not to be regarded as mere brutum fulmen. Day by day, brought to the people of Columbia tidings of newer atrocities committed, and a wider and more extended progress. Daily did long trains of fugitives line the roads, with wives and children, and horses and stock and cattle, seeking refuge from the wolfish fury which pursued. Long lines of wagons covered the highways. Half naked people cowered from the winter under bush tents in the thickets, under the eaves of houses, under the railroad sheds, and in old cars left there along the route. All these repeated the same story of brutal outrage and great suffering, violence, poverty and nakedness. Habitation after habitation, village after village - one sending up its signal flames to the other, presaging for it the same fate - lighted the winter and midnight sky with crimson horrors. . . . Where the families still ventured to remain, they were, in most instances, so tortured by insult, violence, robbery and all manner of brutality, that flight became necessary, and the burning of the dwelling soon followed the flight of the owner. No language can describe the sufferings of these fugitives, or the demonic horrors by which they were pursued; nor can any catalogue furnish an adequate detail of the widespread destruction of homes and property. Granaries were emptied, and where the grain was not carried off, it was strewn to waste under the feet of their cavalry or consigned to the fire which consumed the dwelling. The negroes were robbed equally with the whites of food and clothing. The roads were covered with butchered cattle, hogs, mules and the costliest furniture. Nothing was permitted to escape. Valuable cabinets, rich pianos, were not only hewn to pieces, but bottles of ink, turpentine, oil, whatever could efface or destroy, upon which they could conveniently lay hands, was employed to defile and ruin. Horses were ridden into the houses. Sick people were forced from their beds, to permit the search after hidden treasures. In pursuit of these, the most diabolic ingenuity was exercised, and the cunning of the Yankee, in robbing, proved far superior to that of the negro for concealment. The beautiful homesteads of the parish country, with their wonderful tropical gardens, were ruined; ancient dwellings of black cypress, one hundred years old, which had been reared by the fathers of the republic - men whose names were famous in Revolutionary history - were given to the torch as recklessly as were the rudest hovels; the ancient furniture was hewn to pieces; the costly collections of China were crushed wantonly under foot; choice pictures of works of art, from Europe; select and numerous libraries, objects of peace wholly, were all destroyed. The summer retreats, simple cottages of slight and unpretending structure, were equally devoted to the flames, and, where the dwellings were not destroyed - and they were only spared while the inhabitants resolutely remained in them - they were robbed of all their portable contents, and

> what the plunderer could not bear away, was ruthlessly hewn to pieces. The inhabitants, black no less than white, were left to starve, compelled to feed only upon the garbage to be found in the abandoned camps of the enemy. The corn scraped up from the spots where the horses fed, has been the only means of life left to thousands but lately in affluence. It was the avowed policy of the enemy to reach our armies through the sufferings of their women and children – to starve out the families of those gallant soldiers whom they had failed to subdue in battle.

An under-reported fact is that when Sherman left Columbia, he commanded 248 wagons filled with Southern treasure.

Simms reports more atrocities committed by the invading monsters:

> We have been told of successful outrages of this unmentionable character being practiced upon women [rapes] . . . . Many are understood to have taken place in remote country settlements, and two cases are described where young negresses were brutally forced by the wretches and afterwards murdered – one of them being thrust, when half dead, head down, into a mud puddle, and there held until she was suffocated. . . . We need, for the sake of truth and humanity, to put on record, in the fullest types and columns, the horrid deeds of these marauders upon all that is pure and precious – all that is sweet and innocent – all that is good, gentle, gracious, dear and ennobling – within the regards of . . . Christian civilization.

And then there was the killing:

> [Mayor Goodwyn] while walking with the Yankee General, heard the report of a gun. Both heard it, and immediately proceeded to the spot. There they found a group of soldiers, with a stalwart young negro fellow lying dead before them on the street, the body yet warm and bleeding. Pushing it with his feet, Sherman said, in his quick, hasty manner, "What does this mean, boys?" The reply was sufficiently cool and careless. "The d___d black rascal gave us his impudence, and we shot him." "Well, bury him at once! Get him out of sight!" As they passed on, one of the party remarked, "Is that the way, General, you treat such a case?" "Oh!" said he, "we have no time for courts-martial and things of that sort!"

"Should you capture Charleston, I hope by some accident the place may be destroyed. And if a little salt should be sown upon the site, it may prevent the growth of future crops of nullification and secession." These words advocating the centralization of American government along with the destruction of Charleston came in 1865 from Lincoln's Chief of Staff, Major General Henry Halleck. The message was addressed to Sherman, whose mode of warfare was hailed in Northern papers as genius and decried in the South as barbaric.

Today, our children are taught not to question or to doubt, but to praise and to glorify the so-called great democratic achievements of Sherman in his notorious march through Georgia and South Carolina.

Simms exposes the popular glorification of Sherman, his men, and their march, falsely represented as an army of noble Americans on a democratic adventure, performing a great military feat. In the process of saving this Sacred Union, the romantic myth goes,

American soldiers were outraged by haughty Southern aristocracy and by the oppression of black people, whom the invaders heartily embraced, so on and on the romantic myths go. As a result, the righteous invaders resolved to destroy Southern society once and for all, and thereby bestow on the planet a new birth of freedom.

These absurd pretensions of virtue and self-righteous justifications for criminal acts are easily contradicted by hundreds of Southern sources, chief among them is Simms's account of Sherman in Columbia. Simms reveals Sherman's invasion as evil, as rationalized by a deformed Christianity, as a fatal violation of the Constitution and core American values, and as carried out by a pretentious army of plundering criminals.

CONCLUSION

All it takes for evil to triumph is for good men and women to do nothing. Silence is the greatest shame. We must speak up, no matter how difficult.

To protect the Constitution and the freedom and well-being of the people of the South, the Southern states affirmed the right to disobey the American central government: a right affirmed and established by the founding generation, although labelled treason by Lincoln and his Administration.

As a result of defending the values of the American founders and the rights made explicit in the Declaration of Independence, the South was wrongfully, criminally, and brutally invaded - not by those warring for Christ and Christian morality, not by those building an exceptional civilization in the Western Hemisphere, not by those defending humanity or human rights. The South was invaded, brutalized, and conquered by "monsters of virtuous pretension." As eyewitnesses like Simms said over and over again, by felons and brutes - who not only broke the rules of warfare by attacking, raping and murdering innocent civilians, but who also broke the rules of decency and Christian morality. I remind you that Simms addresses his historical narrative of the destruction of Columbia to Christians, everywhere.

Simms was present throughout this American enormity, when he recorded the horrors of invasion, and Sherman's repeated denials - denials Sherman himself would eventually acknowledge. Simms not only exposes Sherman, but he also rebukes the invaders' virtuous pretensions to defend and to justify their monstrous behavior.

Those who attempted to destroy the South did not succeed (although some are still trying today), because the ideas and ideals of the South are preserved, along with the malignant cruelty of the invaders — preserved in Simms's writings as well as in the writings of many others. Southern ideals are also preserved in the Atlanta art that influenced my youth. What kind of civilization could inspire the Cyclorama, the carvings on Stone Mountain, and the American classic *Gone With the Wind*? These works of art spoke to me as an Atlanta youth, as well as to millions of others. The meaning of great Southern art points to the ideals of the American South.

The ideas and ideals of Thomas Jefferson and the Founding Fathers were both the inspiration and the model of the Southern Confederacy. I was taught that Confederate ideals include the goal of the responsible, sovereign individual, tempered by family, community, church and state. I knew that the Southern Confederacy was intended to protect the Southern land and the rights of the people on that land to be free from arbitrary executive power, entangling alliances, destructive wars, and unfair regional exploitation to benefit sectional elites.

If our teachings are false, if our art like the Cyclorama, Stone Mountain, and *Gone With the Wind* is inferior and irrelevant, and if our literary and historical sources like Simms are wrong, then they will not withstand the onslaught of globalism, secularism, and empire building. But if they are true, then they will sustain us in all manner of dark and threatening times, because we have faith in the final justice of the Good Lord Above and in His ultimate victory. Like our Revolutionary War forefathers, we have faith that freedom will eventually triumph over all forms of tyranny and usurpation. Like our Confederate heroes, we have faith that the courage, sacrifices and patriotism of men like Robert E. Lee, Stonewall Jackson, and William Gilmore Simms will not only endure but will finally prevail.

Lyon Gardiner Tyler and Southern History

Brion McClanahan

THE ATTACK ON THE so-called "lost cause" myth in American history is nothing new. Beginning in the 1950s and 60s, historians like Kenneth Stampp began a concerted effort to undermine the dominant historical interpretation of the War, namely that the War and Reconstruction had been stains on American history, that the War could have been avoided, and that slavery was only a peripheral issue in the entire conflict. Stampp privately wrote that he could never be a "negro-hating Doughface" like James G. Randall or Avery O. Craven, men whom Stampp considered to be some of the worst historians in American history. Why? Because unlike Stampp, Craven and Randall did not buy the neo-abolitionist narrative of the events leading to the War. Craven, in fact, placed the War at the feet of a "blundering generation" too foolish to accept compromise to avoid bloodshed. He had no love for Southerners, but he was equally hard on Northern abolitionists. To Stampp, the War had been a moral crusade from the beginning, a conflict that began when Southerners realized the institution of slavery was doomed and the only recourse was secession. Abolitionists were the morally righteous men in white hats destined to save America from the evil slavocracy. It did not matter that most American viewed abolitionists with suspicion in the antebellum United States, or that their tactics were less than peaceful. What matters is that they won, and the South should be viewed in a far less sympathetic light than the "blundering generation" school accepted.

This is what Stampp had to say to his mentor, William B. Hesseltine, in 1945:

> I'm sick of the Randalls, Cravens and other doughfaces who crucify the abolitionists for attacking slavery. If I had lived in the 1850s, I would have been a rabid abolitionist. When the secession crisis came I would have followed the abolitionist line: let 'em secede and good riddance....But once the war came, I would have tried to get something out of it. I would have howled for abolition, and for the confiscation and distribution of large estates among negroes and poor whites, as the Radicals (some of them) did. I would have been a radical because there was nothing better to be. I couldn't have been a conservative Lincoln Republican and rubbed noses with the Blairs and Sewards; and I couldn't have been a Negro-hating copperhead. My only criticism of the Radicals is that they weren't radical enough, at least so far as the southern problem was concerned.

Stampp, along with Eric Foner and others, are often cited as the "objective" historians in contrast to the "Lost Cause" pro-Southern ideologues. Who is telling the truth, here?

We would be foolish to think that Stampp occupied a novel place among American historians. The early postbellum period was littered with historians ready and willing to make the South the ultimate villain in American history, the "peculiar" other offset by the superior and progressive North. James Ford Rhodes multi-volume work on American history is indicative of this type of scholarship. Rhodes believed Reconstruction to be one of the worst episodes in American history, but he held men like Calhoun and Jefferson Davis responsible for the carnage and bloodshed of the War and placed the institution of slavery front and center. Rhodes was not a neo-abolitionist and minimized the role of abolitionism in the coming of the conflict, but he rejected the Southern position that the War had been fought for the principles of 1776 and the right to self-government. Other historians, like the German Hermann von Holst, took the same approach, which is why Southerners believed, and rightly so, that the real war was only beginning.

The War that ended on the battlefield in 1865 began anew with the pen not long after the ink dried at Appomattox Courthouse. Southerners understood the stakes. If the Northern view of the War, now so triumphantly supported by Lincoln's assassination in 1865, became ingrained into American society, there would be no hope of salvaging any promising memory of the Southern people. They would be traitors identified with an institution that the majority of Americans now found morally repugnant. They knew the real story of America, the fact that Virginia was the most important colony and State in the early federal republic, that the South had led the way for much of American history, that their cause of secession was the same as that of the founding generation, and that there was more than just a smidgen of hypocrisy in Northern self-righteousness in the afterglow of victory. But how do a defeated people retain their memory and their character? More importantly, how do the losers help write the story? And it must be noted that the vicious attacks on traditional Southern history we face today are not novel. Southerners in the postbellum period experienced the same thing.

There were two types of Southern historians in the postbellum period, the amateurs and a burgeoning and productive group of well trained professionals. Both aimed to craft a history of the South untainted by Northern views. The first group included people like Mildred Lewis Rutherford of Athens, GA and John Cussons of Alabama.

Cussons penned two little books on Southern history in the late nineteenth century. For thirty-two years he had watched as "Northern friends of ours have been diligent in a systematic distortion of the leading facts of American history— inventing, suppressing, perverting, without scruple or shame—until our Southland stands to-day pilloried to the scorn of all the world and bearing on her front the brand of every infamy." The South had sat silently, watching as the North explored every avenue to disparage her people, her cause, and her history. In the short period following the War, Northerners had painted the South as the personification of "meanness," "folly," and "utter and incurable inefficiency." The South was the despicable "other" in the American mind, and as a result "The economist with a principle to illustrate, the moralist full of his Nemesian philosophy, the dramatist in quest of poetic justice—in short every craftsman of tongue or pen with a moral to point or a tale to adorn turns instinctively to this mythical, this fiction-created South, and finds the thing he seeks."

This had broken the unwritten agreement between the two sections following the War. Northerners would acknowledge Lee and Jackson as great Americans and in return the South would consider Lincoln to be the man of hour who saved the Union.

And the South had come to accept it. Her people had been turned against their own history, brainwashed into believing the Yankee version of American history, a history fabricated in the years following the great Southern struggle for independence. Southern children were the targets and as a result,

> our grandchildren, trained in the public schools, often mingle with their affection an indefinable pity, a pathetic sorrow—solacing us with their caresses while vainly striving to forget "our crimes." A bright little girl climbs into the old veteran's lap, and hugging him hard and kissing his gray head, exclaims: "I don't care, grandpa, if you were an old rebel! I love you!"

This could have been said today.

Cussons understood one of the great maxims of history by quoting the great British historian Lord Macaulay, "a people which takes no pride in the noble achievements of a remote ancestry will never achieve anything worthy to be remembered by remote descendants." The systematic destruction of the Southern tradition by distortion and lies would render her people impotent in the future. His words were more than quaint "unreconstructed" rants against the government. They were not "I'm A Good Ol' Rebel." Cussons wielded a philosophical hammer against Yankee Puritanism in an attempt to save the South from self-loathing, guilt, and shame.

Cussons knew the South, the real South, still existed. It had been defeated in war, but the Southern people had much to admire in their history. Her heroes defended a noble tradition and that tradition, if correctly articulated and saved, would place the South at its proper place in the forefront of American history. Unfortunately, his double-barreled assault on Yankee distortion has been mostly forgotten. His two short works defending the South are not placed among the great tomes of the late post-bellum period primarily because not many know they existed. *United States "History" as the Yankee Makes and Takes It* and its more substantial sister *A Glance at Current History* are clear, concise, and more importantly caustic. They are as witty as Bledsoe's *Is Davis a Traitor?* or Taylor's *Destruction and Reconstruction* and while not as meaty as Stephens's or Davis's multi-volume masterpieces on the War and Southern history offer the same defense.

Cussons was born in England and emigrated to North America in 1855. He lived for four years among the Sioux in the Northwest where they named him "The Tall Pine Tree." He moved to Selma, Alabama, in 1859 and became a newspaperman as the half owner of the *Morning Reporter.* He opposed secession but when the War began in 1861 he served as a commander of scouts and sharpshooters in the Army of Northern Virginia. He was captured at Gettysburg and after his release spent the remaining months of the War out in the Western theater, eventually fighting with Nathan Bedford Forrest. Following the War he founded a publishing firm, owned a large hunting lodge in Virginia, and served as one of the officers of the United Confederate Veterans.

United States "History" as the Yankee Makes and Takes It was a short work designed to illustrate the growing problem of Puritan history in America. The Puritan, Cussons argued, always considers himself to be the moral superior to any other people. From the beginning, Puritans had formulated the false notion that their customs and traditions produced better men and societies than those of the South. For example, the "Yankee" or "Puritan" idea would logically "formulate and demonstrate" the following proposition:

1. Patrick Henry, furnished with a good stock of groceries, failed at twenty-three.
2. A Puritan, even of the tenth magnitude, under like circumstances, would not fail at twenty-three.

Ergo: A tenth-rate Puritan is the superior of Patrick Henry.

This, of course, is a fallacy in logic but one that makes perfect sense to the New England mind.

Cussons defined the Yankee as thus:

> Self-styled as the apostle of liberty, he has ever claimed for himself the liberty of persecuting all who presumed to differ from him. Self-appointed as the champion of unity and harmony, he has carried discord into every land that his foot has smitten. Exalting himself as the defender of freedom of thought, his favorite practice

> has been to muzzle the press and to adjourn legislatures with the sword. Vaunting himself as the only true disciple of the living God, he has done more to bring sacred things into disrepute than has been accomplished by all the apostates of all the ages....Born in revolt against, law and order—breeding schism in the Church and faction in the State—seceding from every organization to which he had pledged fidelity—nullifying all law, human and divine, which lacked the seal of his approval—evermore setting up what he calls his conscience against the most august of constituted authorities and the most sacred of covenanted obligations, he yet has the impregnable conceit to pose himself in the world's eye as the only surviving specimen of political or moral worth.

Cussons questioned American education, the attempt by the general government–more importantly the Union veterans of the Grand Army of the Potomac–to write a "true" history of the War, and the false narrative that the North had long been opposed to the principles of States' rights, nullification, and secession.

At every step, Cussons defended the men and the cause of the South and lamented that her history was being written by the victors. "The whole story of the war and its causes," he wrote, "has been distorted and perverted and falsely told. Yet at the bar of unbiased history, before the tribunal of impartial posterity, it will become manifest that the vital principle of self-government—the world's ideal, and what was fondly deemed America's realization of that ideal—went down in blood and tears on the stricken field of Appomattox. It was there that Statehood perished. It was there that the last stand was made for the once-sacred principle of 'government by free consent.'" The old republic of the founding generation was buried by Puritanical self-righteousness. Cussons predicted the inevitable outcome:

> Potential classes are now longing for a change; they are earnest in their desire for what they call "a strong government." And it may be that their yearnings will not be in vain. The corruption of a republic is the germination of an empire. A period of domestic turbulence or foreign war would render usurpation as easy as the repetition of a thrice-told tale. Political speculations would then reassume their old names—incivism, sedition, constructive treason—and the familiar remedies would be applied—press censorship, the star chamber, *lettres de cachet,* and bureaus of military justice.

In the final chapter of *A Glance at Current History,* Cussons addressed the relationship between the Indian tribes and the general government and compared the plight of the Indian-harassed, chased, threatened with extermination-with that of the South during and after the War. He recoiled at their treatment and bristled at attempts to make them "good people." How would it sound, he asked, if the Indian said in response to the bloodthirsty General Philip Sheridan that, "There is no good Yankee but a dead Yankee?" Like the South, the Indian had a noble heritage that was being trampled by an invading army. Cussons believed the two shared a common cause.

Like Cussons, Rutherford was not a trained historian, but also like Cussons had a firm grasp of the Yankee problem in postbellum America. Rutherford, however, was a leading figure in the establishment of the United Daughters of the Confederacy and was the historian general of that organization. It is true that Rutherford made mistakes in her histories, and she is often castigated for her "romanticized" version of the antebellum period, particularly of race and slavery (positions that are unfashionable today but were bolstered by the professional historians of the time), but Rutherford also made several good contributions to Southern history most often by using the words of Northerners to support her arguments. Her often vilified *Truths of History* is a collection of primary documents designed to defend the Southern view of government and society with Northern voices. This is an artful tactic that can still be used today.

Rutherford took seriously the concern of author and diplomat Thomas Nelson Page—another vilified figure from the New South—that

> In a few years there will be no South to demand a history if we leave history as it is now written. How do we stand today in the eyes of the world? We are esteemed ignorant, illiterate, cruel, semi-barbarous, a race sunken in brutality and vice, a race of slave drivers who disrupted the Union in order to perpetuate human slavery and who as a people have contributed nothing to the advancement of mankind.

Again, could not the same words be written today? Rutherford insisted that Southerners study their own past to combat what we would call Cultural Marxism today, or the Yankeefication of American history. And Southerners responded. The late nineteenth and early twentieth century witnessed a resurgence of interest in Southern history, particularly from native Southerners. Most, including Rutherford, wanted to place the South as the pivotal section in the founding of the American "nation." As Northerners ran around telling students that the Pilgrims invented American democracy and all great intellectual, cultural, and technological innovations came from the North, Southerners pushed back, with a new breed of professional historians leading the way.

The South in the Building of the Nation series was published in 1909 as both a counterweight to the Northern mythmaking of American history and an affirmation of the South's role in the establishment of the United States. The title gives away the intent of the project. Southerners were not content to be the backwater of American civilization, the "peculiar" others; they were the primary builders of that civilization, from the founding period to the early 20th century. The series can be viewed as a companion to the *Library of Southern Literature* and like that series the editors and contributors to *The South in the Building of the Nation* were a veritable who's who among Southern historians in the early twentieth century. Several university presidents and leading Southern historians participated with no historian born or bred north of the Mason Dixon among the list. Some recognizable contributors and editors include Franklin L. Riley, the founder of the Mississippi Department of Archives and History; U.B. Philips, for a time the pre-eminent American historian on slavery and plantation life in the South; George Petrie, the first Alabamian to earn a Ph.D and the founder of the Auburn University history department, graduate school, and most importantly for many in that state, the Auburn football team; Walter Fleming, a member of the "Dunning School" of Reconstruction and the editor of the important but now out of favour *Documentary History of Reconstruction* among other works; Samuel Chiles Mitchell, president of several universities across the South including that of South Carolina; Edwin Mims, professor of literature at Vanderbilt and primary advisor for almost every one of the Fugitive Agrarians; Douglas Southall Freeman, the distinguished historian and author of multi-volume biographies of Lee and Washington; and two important presidents of the College of William and Mary, J.A.C. Chandler and Lyon Gardiner Tyler, the latter of the two being the focus of a later portion of this talk.

Like many of the histories produced during this period in the South, *The South in the Building of the Nation* is often ridiculed for its open racism and glorification of the Old South, but these attacks are often leveled by people who have never read any of the volumes. Like U.B. Phillips and the Dunning School of historians, they are often flippantly discarded by establishment historians and graduate students while much of the fundamental material has not been disproven only re-interpreted by later generations. That is the key to understanding the current situation. The fight is against *interpretation* not *fact,* and as any honest historian will tell you, most of history is just that, interpretation. The progressive historian Charles Beard, for example, never said he had *the* interpretation of the Constitution, it was *an* interpretation. This is why graduate students used to study historiography. Now they study fashionable trends without digesting who wrote history or why a particular history was written. That is often as important as the material itself. There are, of course, exceptions to this rule. One of the better is John David Smith's *Slavery, Race, and American History* where he criticizes "contemporary scholars" who "pay insufficient attention to the contributions of their intellectual forefathers, especially those with whom they disagree ideologically...."

It is true that most, if not all, of the contributors of this series were "racist," but so was most of America in 1909. They had commonly held views for their time, but the charge of racism is an anti-intellectual statement designed to smother or blacklist a currently unfashionable belief, study, or program. Many of these men were progressives who also viewed the South as an important part of American civilization moving forward. One contributor, Peter J. Hamilton, served as a federal judge in Puerto Rico; another, Colyer Meriwether, was an American advisor in Japan; and Mims became an outspoken opponent of lynching in the South, and later served as president of what is now called SACS, a regional accrediting body for Southern colleges and universities. Several of these men held leadership positions in colleges and universities across the South well into the mid-twentieth century. The history contained in these volumes is perhaps the best expression of the Southern mind in the early postbellum period. That alone should make it worthy of study, but that would also require a careful examination of the material without the lenses of presentism, something the current academic profession seems almost unable or unwilling to do. In short, these volumes cannot simply be written off as some quaint "lost cause" fabrication of American history or a "white supremacist" polemic. They are a serious academic exercise in a solid narrative format, a thorough and at times critical examination of the South's role in the American experience and an attempt to understand all facets of Southern history, political, cultural, and economic with the evidence available to them.

Two volumes, in fact, are dedicated to Southern economics, something that had not been comprehensively studied since the late antebellum period. One section on "Free Contract Labor in the Antebellum South" plowed new ground in telling a sympathetic story of free black labor before the War, a field that in 1909 was virtually non-existent. This section, by the way, was written by Alfred H. Stone of Mississippi, a man now regarded as one of the more virulent racists in the South but in his day was so well received as an economic historian that he was appointed as a research associate at the Carnegie Institute of Washington. The aforementioned Smith wrote a very good essay on Stone in his *Slavery, Race, and American History*.

Yet, while Phillips, Freeman, and Fleming still receive attention from the modern academic community, even if insufficient, one of the contributors to this series, Lyon Gardiner Tyler, has been either ignored or ridiculed by the modern academy and the public at large. The reason? Tyler did not confine his efforts to academic history. He would often engage the popular press—and by engage meaning take them head on when they were wrong—and write histories intended for consumption by the masses. In other words, Tyler took seriously his role as a historian for the people, not just academics. This is what the late Shelby Foote used to tell anyone who would listen. Historians need to learn how to write.

Tyler was the second youngest son of President John Tyler and as such a fervent son of Virginia. In addition to being the President of the College of William and Mary, Tyler spent much of his career writing popular histories of Virginia from the colonial period to the present day. He wrote and edited *Tyler's Quarterly Historical and Genealogical Magazine*, which is a fine collection of articles related to all elements of Virginia history. Some of these works were little more than pamphlets for mass consumption. For example, his "Virginia First," also published at the Abbeville Institute website, is a collection of fifteen points designed to place Virginia at the forefront of American history. As he wrote in his first point,

> The name first given to the territory occupied by the present United States was Virginia. It was bestowed upon the Country by Elizabeth, greatest of English queens. The United States of America are mere words of description. They are not a name. The rightful and historic name of this great Republic is "Virginia." We must get back to it, if the Country's name is to have any real significance.

The rest of the little essay follows this trend. Virginia had the first representative government, the first thanksgiving, was the first to declare independence, the first to agitate for independence, the greatest of the early American statesmen and leaders and gallant sons who served with distinction throughout American history. Tell that to the tour guides at

Plymouth and they will give you a curious look of bewilderment. Don't you know that Plymouth was the first at everything?

Tyler was also responsible for an essay that ran in *Time* magazine in June 1928 entitled "Tyler vs. Lincoln." In April of that year, *Time* ran an article comparing Abraham Lincoln to John Tyler. As you might image *Time* found Tyler to be lacking, calling him "historically a dwarf." It must be understood that modern Lincoln worship and disdain for the South did not begin in the modern age. L.G. Tyler responded in a splendid little rebuttal. Tyler wrote that "real history cares nothing for the blare of trumpets and the shouts of propagandists...." He then surgically sliced apart the Lincoln myth in a way that few historians have been able to do. Tyler wrote,

> In conducting the war Lincoln talked about "democracy" and "the plain people", but adopted the rules of despotism and autocracy, and under the fiction of war powers virtually suspended the Constitution. This surely cannot be said of John Tyler, as president, who, though of parentage much higher in the social scale than Lincoln, was a much greater democrat, since he professed faith in the Constitution and would not violate it, even at the dictation of his party.

Tyler attacked Lincoln's career as a lawyer by claiming that Lincoln made dirty deals and underhanded moves to secure victory for his usually well financed clients. This extended to his political career where Lincoln so vigorously pursued office that he cared little as to how he obtained a seat in Congress, or ultimately, president. Whereas John Tyler assumed the office of president after several brilliant terms as a United States Senator, Lincoln was nominated because he was slick and was able to appeal to everyone and no one at the same time. In other words, Lincoln was a politician and Tyler a statesman. Tyler sought peace and avoided war with Mexico during his administration through expert diplomacy with both the British and the Mexican government, something Lincoln entirely avoided in the time leading to the disastrous conclave through arms between the North and South from 1861-1865. Lincoln professed peace but never showed the resolve to see it through. Tyler, even in 1861, sought peace until it became clear that the Lincoln administration had no interest in a bloodless solution to the conflict. Tyler correctly shows that Lincoln's entire program was directed toward war from the minute he assumed office in March 1861. This would be considered "Lost Cause" mythology today—and several of Tyler's critics have labeled it that—but the evidence is clear that Lincoln went headfirst into war when other options were on the table.

Perhaps the best part of Tyler's piece is his explanation as to *why* the tariff issue was important in 1861. It was not because, as several modern historians like to suggest, the South paid more in tariff revenue than the North, but because the newly crafted Southern tariff would be less than half of the tariff of the general government, thus creating a competitive economic situation that the North would lose. Lincoln was not concerned about "losing his revenue" because Southerners were out of the Union and thus could not buy Northern manufactured goods. He was concerned about "losing his revenue" because the miniscule Confederate tariff would undercut the North and shift trade to the Southern confederacy, thus destroying the Northern economy. We should stop saying "Southerners paid 80 percent of the tariff" and start outlining the real economic motivation behind Lincoln's insistence that the South remain in the Union: Northern financial interests could not compete with a vibrant free trade federal republic on their doorstep. Again, this is written off as a "lost cause" myth and establishment historians can sit on television and make stupid statements like, "No one was talking about the tariff" in 1861 when as Tyler clearly shows they were.

But this is only scratching the surface of Tyler's supposed "lost cause" mythology. According to the critics, Tyler's most substantial contribution to the "lost cause" myth was his 1920 *A Confederate Catechism*. The *Catechism* received quite a bit of press in May of this year with several mainstream and leftist media outlets running pieces on its modern influence or lack thereof. The *Catechism* is still used by some SCV camps as an educational piece and certainly has historical worth. Critics won't agree, but remember, the current assault is over interpretation. The *Catechism* does outline several points that critics view as both illogical and ahistorical, not the least of which is Tyler's minimization of slavery as a cause of the War. It is also denounced because of its format, but most modern academics equate catechisms to solely religious functions, not realizing that many "history textbooks" used a catechism format in the late 19th and early 20th centuries. Matthew Page Andrews, for example, used a catechism format for his very popular United States history textbook, a work that was adopted by hundreds of schools across the United States. Rote memorization was the standard method of historical learning until the 1960s when it fell out of fashion. Better to learn theories and trends than actual people, places, dates, and events, unless of course those people, places, dates, and events correspond to a revised version of America.

Tyler contends that the Northern invasion of the South started the War, that Lincoln purposely broke the peace between North and South when he invaded Fort Pickens—not Sumter—that Lincoln did not wage war to "free the slaves," that the South had long been the "milchcow" of the North and that secession was true "government of the people, by the people, and for the people."

These positions are simply heresy to the Lincoln mythmakers, and accordingly Tyler, like the Southern historians of the early 20th century, has come under attack for being a liar, a mythmaker, and worse a racist.

But this is why the New South needs more attention. Could every one of Tyler's 20 points in his *Catechism* or his 15 points in *Virginia First* be validated? Could modern historians learn from L.G. Tyler, or how about Cussons, or Rutherford, or the dozens of professional historians like Phillips or Fleming, or pro-amateurs like Stone? I think the answer is definitively yes. More importantly, can the New South be as vital to the understanding of the Southern tradition as the Old? Did men like Dabney and Mencken or even the Agrarians fail to entirely understand the influence of the Old on the New? Could the New have prospered without some of the ways of the Old, and was the race question the only element of Southern history in the 20th century that made it unique? In other words, were Southerners just good racist Northerners? In essence, the narrative goes, take away race and Southerners are as bland, corrupt, and money hungry as a New England Yankee, only more violent and with less real culture. It was only race that made them unique. That would seem to be the assumption, but I think a tremendously incorrect one.

My goal has been to pique your interest as historians, philosophers, writers, and scholars in the New South, to seek to understand this period and save it from the clutches of the carpetbagger dominated "Southern Studies" programs that now dot the landscapes of the Southern academy. Their goal is to condemn and "contextualize," to sell a myth to the American public that these Southerners were corrupt and deceitful without remorse or compunction for the sin of secession and sectionalism. Those are modern value judgements, and their myth is even more whimsical than the "lost cause." As Alfred Stone wrote in *The South and the*

Building of the Nation, "Southern history, as told by Southern people, may be full of myths and ill-founded traditions; but, as it has thus far been written by historians of other sections, it is replete with interpretations and conclusions almost fantastic and apparent efforts of the imagination."

The South and The Modern World

Carey Roberts

UNDERSTANDING THE ROLE of the South in the world in which we live is no easy task. Often we approach a topic as vast as "the South in the modern world" through a variety of different avenues where each presents a separate yet convincing case that southerners confronted the problems of modernity in ways unique to their own region and culture. Scholars and learned observers discuss the South's "modern problem" from the standpoint of literary trends, its complex racial dynamics, its food, its music, its religion, and its politics. From each angle, the ultimate goal is for a small portion of the defining features of Southern-ness to build toward a unified whole. Telling a comprehensive story of how all these things fit together to ground Southern life in a vast historical era is far more difficult than producing these short treatments of just one part of Southern culture. Consider the magazines *Southern Living* or *Garden and Gun*, where each collects a series of brief articles on just one example of Southern life whether it be a recipe, a song, a comedian, or a firearm. Readers are to infer what it means to be southern and to readily understand what it is about the South that weaves each of the separate pieces together. Suffice it to say, reversing course and attempting to explain how the inhabitants of one corner of earth - as a whole - made their way through epoch of time that spanned five centuries is not for the faint-hearted.

It should be recognized from the start that painting the South with broad strokes inevitably misses important details. Indeed, it is a common conclusion among scholars and travelers through the South - over the past two centuries - that Southerners flat out rejected the modern world even to this day. According to this common analysis, white Southerners embrace archaic labor systems and racial beliefs rather than accept modern thinking about equality. In the food they eat, Southerners ignore modern nutritional information and dietary warnings. Their music sounds out of place and provincial. Their voting habits remain stubbornly conservative if not reactionary. And the values to which they cling remain unscientific, religious, and hypocritical. It is no wonder that if we define "Modernity" as the period of time in which people invented and imposed rationalized and scientific ideals about how human society ought to work, then Southerners by and large preferred old dogmas over the modern one.

Historians like John Lukacs and Southern observers like Richard Weaver separately observed that as the world passes from the modern age to a new one, it can become easier to see that Southerners did not so much reject modernity and all its ideas, tools, and moral categories as they wished to strike a different sort of balance between these things. In doing so, Southerners from the building of James Fort at the mouth of the James River in 1607 to their staunch support across racial lines of a single presidential candidate in the 2016 election offered a kind of road not taken through modern world.

The first and most lengthy part of this examination is describing modernity - what we mean by modernity. What WE mean by modernity, as part of this association of scholars of the Abbeville Institute, is different from the mainstream treatment of modernity from academics and established intellectuals. The second part of this essay describes where the United States as a whole fits into the stream of modernity with particular focus on the founding era and early colonies with consequential treatment of American society in general. And the third and briefest part focuses on where the South fits into all this. The hope is to leave our readers with something that can provide a sense of encouragement and excitement about the days that are before us, because we live in an unusual time when one age passes into oblivion but we know not what to call the next age to come.

One of the greatest historians of the 20th century, now the 21st century, the late John Lukacs described modernity in a certain way. He understood that modernity began not after but during the Middle Ages. Rather than a sharp division in which there was a renaissance of learning and imagination that freed western civilization from ignorance, Lukacs as well as a host of historians like Regine Pernoud, Norman Cantor, Marc Bloch, Nathan Rosenberg, and L.E. Birdzell Jr. well knew the opposite to be the case.

Most moderns are taught from a young age that the Middle Ages were an era dominated by ignorance. It was a world inhabited by short, fat, squatty people, who ate a lot of bread, and a king, perhaps even a queen, who exercised near absolute power over those poor serfs and peasants that tilled mud for the church and the nobility. In other words, the modern picture of the Middle Ages is one of the "Dark Ages," which itself was a picture that was painted during the Renaissance by people who wanted to present themselves as being better than the era before them. This picture of the Middle Ages is not only erroneous, it is the foundation of many of the mistaken myths that undergird the modern era.

Politically, the Middle Ages were a diverse system, one that was not seen anywhere else in the world at that time. There are some similarities between medieval Europe and medieval Japan, but by and large medieval Europe remained a very distinct place in the world and home to three principle institutions: the crown, the church, and the nobility. The interesting thing about the medieval order is that neither of these three institutions ever commanded absolute power. For the most part, the Middle Ages were a time of overlapping and limiting jurisdictions between these institutions as they competed, not only for power, but also for the hearts, minds, and devotion of medieval Europeans. In other words, in this era, no one institution was greater than the others. No one institution was supreme. They may have claimed supremacy or, as a king, to be designated by God to rule their society. They may have even claimed complete authority over the human soul or complete power over their little "princely" kingdom. But the reality was starkly different. Europe, in the words of the late Ralph Raico, was radically decentralized. It was a conglomeration of over a thousand independent city-states, principalities, papal states, and other forms of medieval kingdoms, not to mention free cities, associations, trade guilds, orders, language groups, dialects, clans, and classes. Neither feudalism nor medieval society as a whole reflected the common picture of a social pyramid capped by one majestic stone. Rather, it resembled a complex celestial constellation, where even the faintest point of light held together vast arrangements of planets, moons, and stars. Medieval Europe consisted of innumerable parallel societies, crossed obligations, feudal responsibilities and corresponding duties. Its complexity astounds the minds of those who best know it.

None of these institutions and divisions provided the means by which any one person could claim complete authority over another person. Even medieval serfs, had they reached a point of absolute duress, had opportunities to flee to a free city, which is why we called these places "free" cities, where serfs could escape the noble obligations imposed upon them. Obviously, this did not always work for everybody, but the opportunity was still there. The complexity of obligations and claims placed upon medieval Europeans, rather than stifling their energy and creativity, often canceled and checked each other. Out of this radically decentralized society emerged much of the greatness that we know as western civilization. This includes important "modern" developments like global trade, science, legal systems, labor exchange, the first banks, savings, and the ability of people to sell their labor for cash and then store and invest that money for future use. Rudimentary industry existed throughout medieval Europe, imaginative art was very much a product of medieval Europe as well, and we seem to forget that the Renaissance resulted from the Middle Ages; in other words, the Middle Ages produced the Renaissance.

The point to be told and one noted by others is that King Street in the Middle Ages looked a lot more like Wall Street today than our popular myths would have us believe. Rather than being a society that was closed by rigid religious tradition, or where political power stayed concentrated in the hands of a few and leaving no room for human liberty, the reality was a very different picture. The Middle Ages produced liberty, the Middle Ages produced freedom.

Again, the success of the medieval order rested in the fact that no one thing, even though it claimed supremacy, was able to exercise supreme control over all. Certainly, examples exist of medieval kings and their champions, as well as lower rulers, who would claim that power. Even Charles the Great's power was never such that would dignify the term "Charlemagne." Something began to happen, however, in late medieval Europe, and it was a slow process that caused a profound change in the way Europeans understood power. It started in a series of wars that medieval kings and princes fought mainly outside of Europe to resist the violent spread of Islam: the Crusades.

Medieval Europeans initiated the Crusades to protect the Christian kingdoms and principalities of the Middle Eastern world from being overrun by Muslim rulers and princes. While in the Middle East, however, the Crusaders came into contact with some things they had yet to understand or even experience. They read about these things from the ancient Greek historians such as Herodotus in his history of the Persian Wars, but they did not quite apprehend them. What the Crusaders came in contact with were oriental forms of government recently imported there by people living in the Middle East. The Spanish had some connection with this in the Iberian Peninsula, but people from other parts of Europe had not. They thus became fascinated with this oriental way of administering society, which was centralized, top-down, and firmly in the hands of a sultan or an emir, who borrowed this form of government from the Indian subcontinent, whose people previously modeled them from what they found in China and the Far East.

Europeans became fascinated with this way of organizing society, and many of the princes who fought in the Crusades and came back to Europe thought they could become as powerful as any oriental despot if they centralized their own kingdoms.

Europeans encountered additional things through the Crusades and subsequent trade with the Orient. While it was not necessarily true that all Europeans were short, squatty, and fat in the Middle Ages, a great many of them actually were, partly because their diet rested heavily upon carbohydrates and bread. They had meat, but grazing patterns and poor breeding resulted in bland meals. Combining European meat with wonderful spices that people in the Middle East imported from the Orient initiated a flavor revolution that swept Mediterranean culinary regions. And so Europeans seeking those spices devised ways of trading with both Middle Easterners and with people in the Orient. This process also exposed Europeans directly with Oriental forms of government, because only governments controlled trade in the Far East. Again, Europeans did not quite understand oriental politics at first. Marco Polo's journals, if read carefully, provide a glimpse of Marco's fascination with Asian administrative forms and Asian political agents. He thought he could just go there and trade with other merchants, but that was not the case.

Finally, from the Crusades and Oriental trade it is but a small stretch to understand how Europeans gained a connection to the new technology of gunpowder and soon mastered its use as a military tool. In many ways, gunpowder was the tool that brought down the entire medieval order because the architectural development of the castle had helped preserve the integrity of all those overlapping jurisdictions of power. One reason why the nobility could resist the encroachments of a king or vice versa, was because they had castles.

Castles were an incredible military tool that protected the radically decentralized institutions of medieval Europe. They prevented any one person or group from consolidating their power. Inside a castle, people could hold themselves up for an extended period of time. They had access to water, and they had access to stored food. Large standing armies had no such ability. Laying siege to castles usually resulted in the army starving and disbursing after quickly exhausting the surrounding area of its resources. Weathering sieges meant castles allowed princes to maintain their separation from control of an overarching, ruling monarch. Yet following the new military applications of gunpowder, the medieval order quite literally crumbled under artillery fire.

The end of medieval order came at the heels of a desire of European kings to emulate the oriental politics they either encountered during the Crusades or confronted through global trade (or at least heard about in the stories of returning crusaders and traders). From this desire to be as strong as oriental power, the medieval world slipped into modernity. As European princes consolidated their power, they expanded their territorial control, subjugated competing sources of power in their areas, and, in short, commenced an all-out assault against the diffusion of power.

There were four principal characteristics of this new modern world for Europeans. The first, and most important characteristic of modernity was the rise of the modern state. Without the modern state, it is difficult to imagine modernity. It ushered in a new political order, whose key institution claimed for itself not a monopoly on power but a right of absolute power, and those are two slightly different things. On the one hand, purveyors of modern state argued it should have *supreme* power, but at the same time, it should also have *all* power. All pockets of resistance must be wiped away.

Modern states emerged by the 14th century, and they quickly consolidated by the end of the late 17th century. Along with the centralization of power, the second key attribute of modernity developed in the form of large, conventional, standing armies. As noted above, in the Middle Ages, large standing armies usually proved ineffectual, because castles could starve off a besieging army. But in the modern era, a large standing army accomplished quite a bit more, particularly in expanding power and territorial control.

A third aspect of modernity was the presence of capitalism. To be clear, capitalism really predates modernity. Capitalism was a function of the late Middle Ages especially in terms of wage labor, investment, banking, and global trade.

But in the modern world, a loose, tenuous relationship developed between capitalist economic exchange and the rise of the modern state's monopoly on power. Nation-states accelerated the development and expanded the reach of capitalism because it fueled the state's expansion through the ability to raise high taxes, field large armies, and steer the development of science toward avenues advantageous to one country over another. All the while, the increase of trade expanded the general wealth of Europeans and thus their ability to pay heavier taxes than before.

Notably, both late medieval Europeans and modern Europeans shared an appreciation for wage labor and emerging industry. Capitalism sustained large populations in ways that the medieval order could not, and so Europeans were careful not to extinguish capitalism, or end free economic exchange, at least not until the late 19th and early 20th century. They wished to steer capitalist development not liquidate it.

A fourth characteristic of modernity is the rise of ideology. Rather than simply being a synonym for "ideas," ideology is a special way of thinking about things. It is a rationalistic, closed system of thought designed to explain all of human behavior through simple precepts. All things in existence are interpreted and explained through the lens of this closed system of belief. Typically, ideological thinking reduces human phenomena and agency to one cause or motivation (power, patriarchy, racial superiority, gender superiority, etc.) and usually rests upon a universal and unfolding sequence of events. For ideologues, history is a series of stages characterized by the singular motivations of the powerful exploiting the powerless. The major difference between modern ideologies depends upon the motivation, which could be class consciousness, gender identity, racial superiority, national will, or other material conditions.

Ultimately, ideology – the way moderns think - is an obsession with power. All modern ideologies are going to insist that power abhors a vacuum and must have one person, one thing, or one idea supreme over everything else. There must be something in charge of human interaction, or it results in anarchy and exploitation. Undergirding every "ism" is an insistence that someone must be in charge. And this is even true of ideological forms of conservatism and liberalism despite efforts by their followers to deny that their way of thinking is ideologically driven. Over time, the modern intelligentsia, who fantasize about everything - in ideological fashion - as forms of power, subsequently began idolizing those institutions that exercise power. In turn, intellectuals produced ideas that best placed them in relationship to those powerful institutions and vicious cycle of corruption starts - hence Lord Acton's famous phrase, "power tends to corrupt, and absolute power corrupts absolutely."

One particular ideology supported the modern era more than the rest. There was "one -ism" that ruled them all and served as a ring of power to unite all aspects of modern thought. It was not communism, nor fascism, nor even liberal democracy. The dominant ideology of modernity was *nationalism.* A group of people became modern when they began thinking nationalistically. And they began to think nationalistically when they started designing political and cultural institutions with the sole purpose of monopolizing a people's devotion and allegiance. It is not the same as patriotism or even cultural conservatism where one's own way of life is loved most. In those traditional forms of devotion, other habits and social forms can be tolerated and even endorsed from a distance. But one's home and place hold priority. In this light, antebellum Southern intellectuals seeking to strengthen Southern cultural identity like William Gilmore Simms could say that Southerners were the best Americans when they were the most Southern. They could love both the South and America as long as they were free to love the South the most. That is not the same thing as nationalism, which is the ideological insistence that devotion to the nation can have neither shared love nor competition.

In no small way, the fragile embrace Southerners made with nationalism as it developed in America during the 19th and 20th century illustrates their different path through the modern era. It was not a rejection of modernity in the way the old noble elite of

Europe resisted the collapse of feudalism or how non-European peoples resist modernization. As Eugene Genovese often explained, Southern conservatives did not reject science, technology, market economies, or even large political institutions. They rejected the obsession with these things done to create a national religion that used science, technology, capitalism, and the federal government to remove all cultural obstacles to one American ideal.

By the 20th century, American nationalism became an acute catalyst of modernity and political consolidation. Yet, this differed from the kind of centralization carried out in prior centuries. For example, many of the early Federalists championed the adoption of the United States Constitution to render government operations more efficient and effective than under the Articles of Confederation. Over the course of the next century, this remained a key and successful political argument. Yet, efficiency in organizing social and economic interaction differed greatly from 20th century arguments about politics being the all-sufficient substitute for other human relationships. Indeed, for Progressive nationalists, the highest and most fulfilling form of human relations culminated in politics. In turn, American intellectuals and leaders measured human worth not through a person's character, actions, or even that they had worth as beings formed in the likeness of God. Instead, the value of human life depended upon the degree to which one engaged in the political system. To remain outside of politics diminished a person's humanity. This connection between worth and power should not be overlooked when surveying the progression of American thought in the 20th century. For moderns, all relationships are rooted in power and indeed exist not because of love or friendship but because of some power relationship. It naturally followed that nationalist ideology - modern ideology - justified the belief that the pure expression of one's humanity culminated in acts of political power. By the end of modernity, the restraint of political power or even the mere mention of political limits proved anathema to ideological definitions of what it meant to be human.

One can easily imagine why traditionally minded Americans, Southerners included, reacted to such a bizarre reading of human existence. Where was friendship? Where was love? Where were the habits of common life that required decency and honor irrespective of how well people knew or even liked each other? At times Southerners reacted to this modern turn of events with great anger and resistance. At other times they reacted with humility, love, and a great deal of humor. Stories of old, music of the heart, and acts of memory and appreciation of the past sustained southern ways of life and cushioned the blows of ideological thinking. And more often than not, Southerners held on to patterns of orthodox Christian devotion. To paraphrase, M.E. Bradford, Southerners survived the worst consequences of modernity by relying upon the same habits, prejudices, and values that caused them to miss the worst aspects of the industrial revolution.

The distinguishing feature of old America - what made it truly exceptional in the early modern world - was the absence of any person or institution that could command the complete loyalty of everything else. Unlike oriental dynasties, would-be absolute monarchs, or fascist and communist governments of the 20th century, no one person or thing could command all the rest. No institution or person was sovereign. As a result, colonial America, distant as it was from the supposed sovereign of the English crown, reflected a medieval rather than modern order. Social institutions overlapped as did economic connections. Religious institutions and landed elites could not command the level of deference enjoyed by their counterparts in the Old World. Political forces tried to transplant social orders in the colonies but failed at every turn. Indeed, efforts to impose any manner of preconceived, rationally designed social order upon colonial societies failed one after another. What seemed to some to be social collapse and spiritual decline reflected the expansion of countless parallel societies and human relationships spread across millions of square miles of shifting political, economic, and cultural frontiers.

Despite centuries of religious and ideological campaigns to rid the South of these parallel societies and render it orderly and properly modern, such efforts fell far short. Now we witness before our eyes the ending of modernity. It is passing before us. Political centralization and problem solving are now financially and mathematically unsustainable. Is there any common blueprint that Americans willingly accept as a model for how they ought to live? Even in the most extreme cases of political correctness, the result, intended or not, is affirmation of ethnic identity, social deviancy, or recognition of unending struggles between factions and groups. That is to say, everything is now about power and nothing is left to appeal to all but the basest and most primitive human emotions. For modern ideologues, nothing even seems human anymore about humanity. There is no vital center because that would require the capacity to love. Moderns, it seems, lost that ability long ago. Southerners did not.

At its heart, the Southern tradition rests on an insistence that human freedom - our relationships with each other, our communities, our neighborhoods, our bands of human interaction outside of politics - is more important than any form of human liberty. What gives meaning to life is not the unfettered soul liberated from social connections and constraint. Liberty of the individual means nothing without the liberty of associations that makes life worth living.

Southerners have great promise in the world to come. Southerners are going to do remarkably well as modernity vanishes, because modernity, with its emphasis on centralization, machines, political consolidation, the emphasis on management of ideas and gizmos are, frankly, not things that Southerners did especially well. Yet as that world vanishes, those things with which Southerners mastered long ago and remain ingrained in their daily culture will likely be the principal means of earthly success in the next era to come.

At one point in the 1990s, Southerners held almost every major political position in the presidential line of succession. This included President Bill Clinton, Vice-president Al Gore, Speaker of the House Newt Gingrich, President Pro Tem Strom Thurmond, and so on. Southerners exercised enormous political influence even if some of them demonstrated at times exactly the ideological thinking common to modernity. Not coincidentally, "political correctness" and a tide of political fanaticism quickly erupted by the turn of the 21st century. Yet, despite the quick rejection of Southern political leadership by the American media and intelligentsia as treacherous and unpropitious, Southerners exercised considerable economic leadership. At one point, the CEO of Walmart was from North Carolina; the CEO of Apple Computer was from Mobile, Alabama; and the CEO of Exxon was from Wichita Falls, Texas. The world's largest companies in terms of capitalization, profit, revenue, and employees were all run by Southerners. What accounts for these two separate periods of Southern political and financial prominence? Could it be that there is something about Southerners, coming as they do from a world of parallel societies, that gives them a special ability to live in a world without a dominate idea or crowned political elite?

If so, then as the modern era comes to a close, perhaps Americans and the world will take notice of how Southerners live, learn, love, and play. Perhaps by default as the one path we followed through Modernity fades into the mists of time, we will once again return to a path laid by Southerners but not taken by Americans. On that day, being most Southern will mean being the best American.

About the Authors

Dr. David Aiken has been Professor of English at the College of Charleston and Charleston Southern University and president of the William Gilmore Simms Society.

Dr. Boyd D. Cathey has a Ph.D from the University of Navarra, Spain, and is a prolific contributor to historical and religious journals in English, French, and Spanish. He has recently published *The Land We Love: The South and Its Heritage.*

The late **William Cawthon** was a founder of the Southern Heritage Association and a William Gilmore Simms scholar.

Dr. Tom Daniel is a college band director and a writer and lecturer on Southern music.

Dr. John Devanny is a teacher, historian, and essayist.

Dr. Richard Gamble is Professor of History and Political Science at Hillsdale College. He is the author of *In Search of a City on a Hill, War for Righteousness,* and *A Fiery Gospel.*

Dr. Paul Gottfried is a prolific author and social critic, president of the H.L. Mencken Club, and Emeritus Professor of Humanities at Elizabethtown College.

Paul C. Graham is co-founder and Executive Director of Shotwell Publishing and the author of *Confederaphobia* and other works.

Ben "Cooter" Jones is an actor, author, and public figure. He is best known from his portrayal of "Cooter" on the popular "Dukes of Hazzard" television series and his service in Congress as Representative from Georgia.

The late **Dr. Thomas H. Landess** was a Professor of English, a student, friend, and follower of the Southern Agrarians, and a prolific author and lecturer. See his recent collection *Life, Liberty, and Lincoln: A Tom Landess Reader.*

Dr. Donald Livingston is Emeritus Professor of Philosophy at Emory University and founder and president of the Abbeville Institute. He is the author of *Philosophical Melancholy and Delusion* and editor of *Rethinking the American Union for the 21st Century.*

Dr. Brion McClanahan is the author of six books on American history and is the founder of McClanahan Academy.

Michael Martin is a teacher and historian and recently the author of *Southern Grit: Sensing the Siege at Petersburg.*

James Rutledge Roesch is an independent historian and recently published *From Founding Fathers to Fire Eaters: The Constitutional Doctrine of States Rights in the Old South.*

Dr. Carey Roberts is Dean and Professor of History at Liberty University and editor of a scholarly edition of William Gilmore Simms' *Captain John Smith.* He is a board member for the scholarly journals *Anamnesis* and *Nomocracy in Politics.*

Dr. Samuel C. Smith is Professor and Chairman of the History Department at Liberty University and the author of *A Cautious Enthusiasm: Mystical Piety and Evangelicalism in Colonial South Carolina.*

Karen Stokes, Archivist for the South Carolina Historical Society has published a dozen works, both history and fiction.

Ryan Walters is the author of *The Last Jeffersonian: Grover Cleveland and the Path to Restoring the Republic* and *Remember Mississippi* and teaches at El Centro College in Dallas.

Clyde N. Wilson is Emeritus Distinguished Professor of History of the University of South Carolina, editor of *The Papers of John C. Calhoun,* and M.E. Bradford Professor of the Abbeville Institute.

The late **Aaron Wolf**, Master of Divinity, was Executive Editor of *Chronicles: A Magazine of American Culture.*

Available From the Abbeville Institute Press

James Everett Kibler

The Classical Origins of Southern Literature

This work explores the continuation of the Classical literary tradition in Southern literature from the Colonial era to the present. It contrasts American writing outside the South which attacked or consciously undermined the Classics with a Southern literature that staunchly adhered to the eternal verities of the Classical tradition.

The work treats both major and minor Southern writers throughout her four centuries. This continued influence is responsible for the global interest in Southern literature.

D. Jonathan White, ed.

Northern Opposition to Mr. Lincoln's War

If you have ever wondered how northerners reacted to the War to Prevent Southern Independence, this collection of essays sheds light on that subject. A collection of essays by scholars of the war: by John Chodes, Marshall DeRosa, Richard Gamble, Brion McLanahan, Allen Mendenhall, Joe Stromberg, Arthur Trask, Robert Valentine, D. Jonathan White. Topics include religion, Copperheads, Oliver Morton, President Franklin Pierce, New York Draft Riots, dissent in Delaware and Philadelphia. Footnotes contain scholarly apparatus.

ABBEVILLEINSTITUTE.ORG

Made in the USA
Columbia, SC
19 December 2020

29381588R00147